MY 5 MINUTE *Happiness* JOURNAL

ixia PRESS

GARDEN CITY, NEW YORK

Graphic design by Cinzia Chiari
Images: ©stock.adobe.com

Copyright © 2019 by Giunti Editore S.p.A., Firenze-Milano
www.giunti.it

This Ixia Press edition, first published in 2024, is a modified
English translation of *Il Mio Diario Della Felicità in 5 Minuti*,
originally published in Italian by Giunti Editore, Milan, in 2019.

ISBN-13: 978-0-486-85349-9
ISBN-10: 0-486-85349-7

Publisher: Betina Cochran
Senior Acquisitions Editor: Fiona Hallowell
Managing Editorial Supervisor: Susan Rattiner
Production Editor: Gregory Koutrouby
Copy Editor: Vali Tamm
Cover Designer: Asya Blue
Creative Manager: Marie Zaczkiewicz
Interior Designer: Jennifer Becker
Production: Pam Weston, Tammi McKenna, Ayse Yilmaz

IXIA PRESS
An imprint of Dover Publications

Printed in China
85349701   2024
www.doverpublications.com

TABLE OF CONTENTS

MANY WAYS TO
take care of yourself
and
BE HAPPIER!

INTRODUCTION

How many times have you started to keep a journal and then abandoned it, because you found you couldn't manage it as you would have wanted to, be it for lack of time, lack of concentration, or because you were simply too tired to write in the evening? Or maybe you've never tried your hand at writing because the sight of a blank page scares you, or because you don't feel you have an aptitude for it; maybe you think it's a waste of time or too much of a commitment to take on when your days already feel crammed with obligations and deadlines?

This Happiness Journal is unlike all others because it provides a user-friendly framework with which, by committing to dedicate just five minutes each morning to your well-being, you'll be able to set off on the right foot on your day's journey toward happiness.

We all know that the most effective way to achieve one's goals is to develop good habits. We also know that gratitude can be a powerful boost in life, but we often fail to appreciate all that we have. Simply put, it is so easy to be distracted by the daily grind, by our rushed routine and commitments, that we fail to notice all we have, and therefore are unable to experience satisfaction for all the beautiful things that happen to us, for the objectives we have achieved, for all that we've created through sheer hard work.

We're always in a hurry; we've scarcely completed one activity before we embark on the next, never giving ourselves the time to take in a deep breath and observe the world, both outside and inside ourselves.

This journal, to be completed over the course of a six-month period of your choice, will help you reflect on yourself and your life, briefly but consistently and effectively, thanks to a very simple method that requires only five minutes of your time per day.

HOW TO USE
this Happiness Journal

Each page of the journal corresponds to a day of the year and is divided into two sections: the *morning routine* and the *evening routine*. You'll fill one page out every day, completing three simple prompts before starting the day and before going to sleep at night.

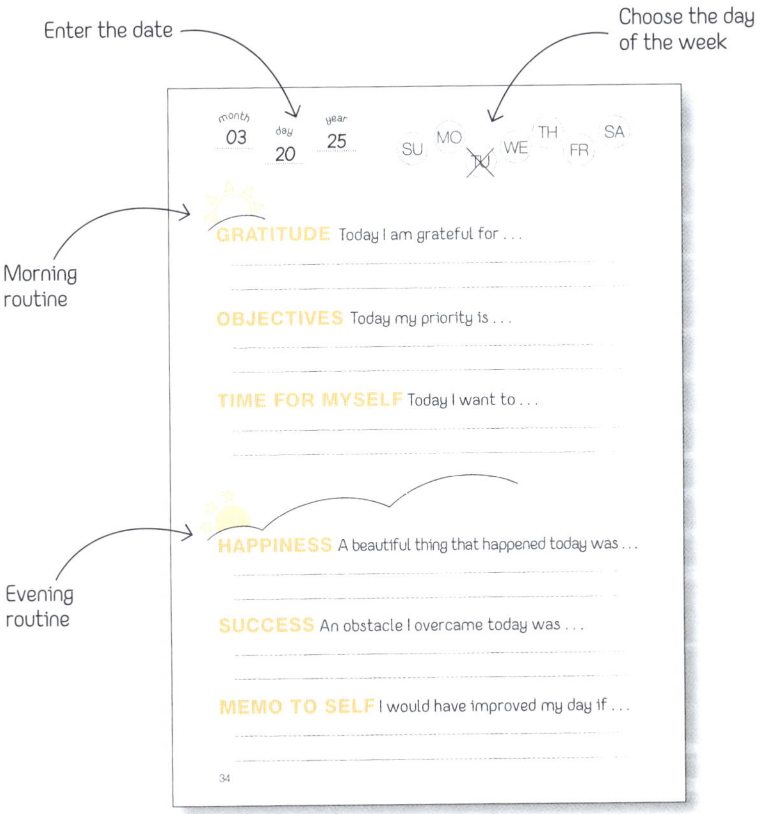

Enter the date

Choose the day of the week

Morning routine

Evening routine

HOW TO USE this Happiness Journal

MORNING ROUTINE

The Morning Routine section includes three open prompts that will help you focus on the positive things in your life and plan your day from a serene perspective. This way, as soon as you wake up, you'll start your day with the right attitude and set a proactive mood for it.

GRATITUDE

Today I am grateful for . . .

This prompt encourages you to focus on a beautiful aspect of your life. It can be something broad and generic, like your family, your children, your four-legged friend, good health, or a beautiful home, etc., or it can be something more specific, such as having enjoyed a pleasant evening on the previous day, having met up with someone special, or having plans to do so over the course of the upcoming day. Alternatively, you can simply feel grateful for a beautiful sunny day or for the smile of the person next to you when you wake up. Feel free to write whatever comes to you, without thinking about it too much; what is important is not so much *what* you write, but that you do it *every* morning, spontaneously and instinctively. This will help you become aware of how many things you usually take for granted, things that are often the most important and valuable.

For instance, you might write;

. . . having slept well, or

. . . having a job I love.

HOW TO USE this Happiness Journal

OBJECTIVES

Today my priority is . . .

This prompt invites you to set priorities for the day and take action to make these things happen. The priorities may be individual or multiple and may relate to your work, your personal life, or both. For example, you might set some deadlines for yourself to help you complete some projects at work, solve a work or family problem, make an important appointment, finally get to the gym after work, or call your mother. What matters is to focus on specific goals, two at the most, so as not to waste energy rushing about between too many commitments for one day.

For example, you might write:

. . . to complete the project that is due today, or

. . . to go out to eat with my friend Julia.

TIME FOR MYSELF

Today I want to . . .

This prompt is the most important of the day, because it reminds you to take care of yourself: the idea is to carve out a little time each day to do something for yourself that you usually wouldn't. The key is not so much to decide to do something extraordinary, but rather something simple that can nevertheless give you a new perspective and do you some good: for example, try a new restaurant, take a different route home from work, decide to have breakfast in your favorite café, wake up early to allow yourself the extra time to take a relaxing shower, decide not to check your smartphone before you get to work, or take a walk in a park you don't usually frequent.

For example, you might write:

. . . go for a ride downtown after work, or

. . . avoid checking my smartphone during dinner.

EVENING ROUTINE

At the end of the day, return to the page you began to work on in the morning, and complete the last three prompts.

HAPPINESS

A beautiful thing that happened today . . .

Our happiness depends not only on what is beautiful, but also on being aware of it. You might appreciate having seen a beautiful sunset, having met someone, or having done well on an exam. Even if something unpleasant happened to you, try to notice even a small thing that made you smile or that you liked; this will help you overcome difficulties and anxiety.

For example, you might write:

. . . was that I worked on an interesting project, or

. . . was that my son received a good grade at school.

HOW TO USE this Happiness Journal

SUCCESSES

An obstacle that I have overcome today . . .

This prompt is fundamental, because it helps you become aware of your successes, large or small, reminds you of a step in the right direction you have taken, of an obstacle that you have managed to overcome. This, in addition to being a source of satisfaction, can also generate a sense of reassurance for the future, because it teaches you that you can get by, that you can deal with anything and, maybe, one day you'll even be able to do so without being overcome by anxiety. You may have excelled at a task that had been worrying you, delivered a project on time that you thought you could not complete, or you may have found a way to solve a problem that only yesterday seemed insurmountable: give yourself credit for these accomplishments. While it is important to learn from one's mistakes, it is also important to learn from one's successes.

For example, you might write:

. . . is that I solved a problem for a customer, or

. . . is that I made peace with George!

MEMO TO SELF

I would have improved my day if . . .

The last prompt encourages you to rethink the day in a self-critical way, to help you avoid making the same mistakes again; it allows you to identify the areas in which you can do better. Maybe you could have been kinder to someone, or smiled back at them, been more focused at work. Alternatively, you might have faced a family situation differently, managed your emotions better, or simply have had more confidence in your abilities. This part of the journal calls for unequivocal sincerity. Do not deceive yourself: facing up to reality and being aware of what you need to do better, will allow you to grow and improve yourself.

For example, you might write:

. . . I had been better able to justify my actions, or

. . . I had wasted less time on futile things.

It will take you only five minutes a day to fill in the journal, and it will be very easy to turn this into a good habit: just keep the journal on your bedside table with a pen on hand. We all have five minutes, so . . . no excuses!

CHANGE your outlook and create GOOD habits

The thought of changing our outlook and habits can be daunting. It's not easy to figure out where to begin when we don't even know exactly what it is that we're trying to accomplish, especially as there is no single "right" path to follow; each one of us has to find our own way.

But it's important to learn to take care of yourself by focusing on the small things. Sometimes a situation can seem so overwhelming, that you're best off tackling it one small step at a time. Set yourself a single goal and complete it: you'll soon realize it was easier than you thought, and you'll feel much better for having completed it!

Begin the process of building a new you right here: try to set achievable priorities for yourself, and deal with each one well before moving on to the next. It won't take long to establish good, new habits; it's enough to start one small step at a time, without exaggerating or expecting to change everything on the first day.

LIVE EACH DAY TO THE FULLEST

Are you too one of those people who suffer from Monday morning syndrome? Do you spend the whole week waiting for the weekend to arrive and the whole year waiting for the holidays? If so, it's too bad, because it's precisely the ordinary days, the ones marked by work and family commitments, by a monotonous stream of duties, that make up the largest part of our lives. It would be such a pity to "write off" such a significant portion of your life.

Consider, instead, your daily routine: is there anything about it you find pleasant? Is there anything you could be doing differently? Try to live every single day well, learn to be aware of, and appreciate, your ordinary activities, the details of your day. This way, you'll learn to appreciate the magic hidden in small things, such as the scent of fresh bed linens, a task brought to completion, or the sunlight filtering through your window. This mindfulness will help you figure out what changes you can implement to lessen the burden of your obligations.

FIVE MINUTES TOWARD FEELING A GREATER SENSE OF SATISFACTION AND HAPPINESS

Writing in the journal every day is imperative. Only by doing so will you reap the benefits. Even if, initially, it might seem of no use to you, if you devote a few minutes a day to it, you'll notice, as the weeks go by, that your attitude has become more positive and that you're more motivated. You'll begin to appreciate things you thought were insignificant, those that you didn't pay attention to before, and that you only began to notice once you were filling in the journal. You'll come to understand the things that make you feel good, and you'll no longer feel so weighed down by worries and obligations. You'll also start to be able to put some of your problems in perspective and feel you've shed some of the emotional baggage that previously weighed you down so much, preventing you from moving forward with the right amount of motivation. Consequently, you'll feel calmer and more balanced, more satisfied, and happy.

The real secret to being happy, to appreciating one's life, and feeling good about oneself—while also remaining open to improvement and growth—is taking care of oneself. Too often, we're overwhelmed by commitments, by the myriads of things we have to do, so we live in a state of perpetual hurry and don't allow ourselves the time to slow down for a moment and come up for air. The most precious asset we have is time, but we often don't realize it, because we're so preoccupied with our daily routine that we get caught up in a vicious circle, dragging on and on without ever living fully, without enjoying the present moment and being able to reflect on ourselves and our surroundings. We have to learn to slow down, to take a break from time to time, and carve out the time to live and not be content with merely *surviving*.

To get out of this rut, to learn to take care of yourself, all you have to do is concentrate on small daily steps: start by committing to set some time aside just for you each day; give yourself this gift of "me time" during which you can indulge your every whim, even if it's just for five minutes. This will allow you to promote your well-being and achieve great results.

Below, you will find advice and suggestions on small things you can do for yourself, organized into five sections:

1. Take a relaxation break

2. Change up your routine

3. Do a digital detox

4. Take care of yourself and others

5. Learn "first-aid" tricks for "off" days

Of course, these are only some suggestions you can decide to adopt or not; ultimately, everyone has to find their own way of taking care of themselves, based on their own personal needs and tastes.

Are you ready for the challenge? All you need to do is start!

Take a
RELAXATION BREAK

In this section, you'll find lots of ideas about how to take a relaxing break, how to switch off and enjoy a moment to yourself. We're so used to running about and juggling numerous things simultaneously that the thought of just a moment of relaxation seems an overly indulgent luxury to us. Instead, it has been scientifically proven that even brief moments of rest during the day are not only restorative but also promote productivity, lucidity, and creativity.

HAVE A SPECIAL BREAKFAST

Wake up ten minutes earlier than usual and go out for breakfast to your favorite café, so you can sit calmly, enjoy sipping your coffee, and read the paper.

This advice applies to any day you need it, but it can be especially useful on days that promise to be particularly difficult, when the week seems like it will never end, and when you 're overwhelmed because you know you won't have a moment to yourself until evening. It may seem counterintuitive but, in reality, those minutes that you might think you are "wasting" will prove to be most valuable in recharging your energy so that you're better able to take on anything that comes at you next.

A SONG FOR YOU

If you're overwhelmed by the things you have to do,
take a short break and listen to a song you love.
Take a deep breath and don't think of anything else.

It's a well-established fact that music has the power to make us relax and can affect our mood. Whether you're at work, running errands, or at home, if you feel overwhelmed by your worries, immerse yourself in the lyrics of a song you love to "switch off" and disconnect from reality for a few minutes. Abandon yourself to the rhythm of the melody; if you're alone and you like, you might even sing: just a few moments will invigorate you.

LEARN TO SAY NO

When you're overwhelmed with demands,
learn to say *No* and take some time for yourself.

Reschedule an appointment, or cancel something you were supposed to do: it's not a disaster. It won't be the end of the world, either, if you postpone replying to an email to the following morning or simply put off completing a task to another day. You mustn't think only about pleasing others; sometimes you need to learn to say *Yes* to yourself, to put yourself first. There's no need to feel guilty: there will always be things to do that are "urgent," but they won't always actually be that important. Learn to be more discerning and to prioritize yourself, so you can carve out a few vital minutes for yourself even on the most hectic days.

TAKE A LONG SHOWER

Treat yourself to a hot comforting shower with perfumed essential oils. Let the streaming hot water relax you for a few minutes and then dry off with soft and clean towels.

Make a restorative shower part of your routine. It won't be the few extra minutes of your time this will take to cause you to be late: slowing down and treating yourself to some comfort are ways to show yourself some love, to give yourself a chance to "reset" so you are better equipped to take on whatever comes next.

TAKE A WALK

Before returning home from work,
take a walk somewhere that relaxes you,
breathing deeply and concentrating on every single step,
without thinking about anything.
Your errands can wait.

It will only take a few minutes; it's not so much a matter of how long you walk but how. You can walk through a park or a tree-lined street to feel in touch with nature, or you can also simply walk along a street you love. Walk slowly, step by step, and notice how your breathing changes as you find your rhythm. At first, focus only on your steps, then gradually look up at the sky and notice whether it's clear or overcast, how bright it is, and with what hues its light is tinged. Notice whether planes or birds are flying overhead. It'll help you clear your mind and feel lighter.

TAKE A RELAXATION BREAK

BREATHE IN

Set aside two quiet minutes,
whether at home or at work,
and focus exclusively on your breathing.

Have you ever felt as if you didn't even have time to breathe, as if you were literally being suffocated by all you had to do? Take a deep breath, for at least six to eight seconds, and then slowly exhale for just as long. Repeat this pattern for at least two minutes, being mindful only of the sound of the air coming into and leaving your breathing passageways. Eventually, you may be able to extend this routine for up to ten minutes, but the important thing is to do this exercise whenever you need it, to deliver oxygen to the brain and keep all thoughts momentarily at bay.

HAVE A GOOD TIME!

You're never too old to play and have fun!
So, do something for no better reason than because you simply
like doing it and it makes you feel good.

When we play, we stimulate our imagination and creativity and feel free to enjoy ourselves just for the sake of it. Rediscover the happiness that comes with getting on a see-saw for a few minutes, or using some colored pencils to draw whatever comes to your mind. Kick or toss a ball about for a while, or go wild dancing and singing a song that you like at the top of your lungs. Feeling like a child again, even for a moment, can have surprisingly beneficial effects: try it!

Change up
YOUR ROUTINE

Another way to take care of yourself and take in a breath of fresh air while you are at it is to change up your habits, break the usual routine, and do something new. This doesn't have to involve anything major; sometimes all it takes is to leave your comfort zone, to deviate from your usual routines to find you've turned your day around and opened yourself up to a whole series of new and exciting opportunities. Don't waste your energy on overambitious or extreme goals, like parachuting or heading for a destination on the other side of the world, but make a list of small, achievable goals, and organize them according to your priorities, so you can check them off one by one as you achieve them.

CHANGE YOUR DAILY COMMUTE

Take an alternate route home from work,
or choose to go on foot or by bike, instead of by car.

We all tend to develop routines for our days and then to stick to them, subconsciously, even if there is no need to. One way we do this is by always taking the same route to and from work. Try going a different way for once, or getting there by a different method: you might discover interesting places, meet someone new along the way, or find out that the new way is much more pleasant than the old one and is even faster!

Change up YOUR ROUTINE

AN OUT-OF-THE-ORDINARY LUNCH

Take a different lunch break:
try that new bistro you've noticed, take a longer lunch break,
or go for a walk instead of sitting down to eat.

Who said that lunch breaks should always be the same? Take control of your day and allow yourself an unplanned treat. Forget cafeteria food or a lunch bag you brought from home, and treat yourself instead to a nice meal out in a place you've never tried before. If the weather's nice, you could even get some good take-out food and eat it outdoors or meet up with a friend for a meal.

EXPERIENCE SOMETHING NEW

When you go out to eat,
order a dish you've never tried before,
or do your grocery shopping in a new place.

Have you ever tasted *crudo*? Have you ever tried ethnic cuisine? Have you been intrigued by an unusual offering on a restaurant menu but then found you just couldn't get yourself to order anything but your go-to favorite dishes? Let down your hair for once and try something new so you can experience different flavors. Food plays an important role in our self-care, and it's essential that we vary it: do your grocery shopping in a new supermarket and allow yourself to find different products. You might be surprised to find you are spending even less than usual!

TAKE UP A SPORT

Be brave and take up a new sport:
instead of going to the gym as usual, go for a swim,
sign up for a dance or yoga class or . . .
why not try out rock climbing?

Physical activity is very important for both physical and mental well-being, but we often limit our choice of exercise to what we're already in the habit of doing, instead of considering the many other types of exercise there are. Trying a new type of exercise can stimulate us and open us up to new perspectives. So try a completely new sport, start playing and you'll be surprised by the benefits that come with new discoveries and new knowledge.

A PINCH OF MADNESS

For once, abandon yourself to your emotions
and act on the impulse to give in to a whim.

Choose something small that you haven't yet dared to do and dare to do it. You could get your hair cut in a new style or dye it a different color, treat yourself to an out-of-town trip on a Sunday to a randomly chosen place, or go out an hour before work just to take a nice walk, relax, and get in touch with yourself. Alternatively, you could make some modifications to a small part of your house to make it feel new: just rearrange some of the furniture or buy some colorful cushions to spruce it up a bit!

Change up **YOUR ROUTINE**

STIMULATE YOUR CURIOSITY

Let yourself be guided by instinct
and savor the taste of discovery
and adventure whenever you can.

You don't need to go far to be stimulated—all you have to do is leave the house and observe your surroundings with a spirit of genuine curiosity. You'll find interesting people, animals, buildings, plants, flowers: all kinds of stimuli. Try to look at them in detail, taking a "mental photograph" of them: are there things you never noticed before? This simple exercise will make you consider things from a new perspective and broaden the limits of your usual thoughts.

MODIFY YOUR SCHEDULE

If you find you're always in a hurry in the morning,
try setting your alarm to ten minutes earlier than usual
and commit to getting up as soon as it goes off.

Simply changing your schedule can make a big difference in your day. Because our bodies are accustomed to a given routine, our brain perceives every little change, no matter how insignificant it is, and this can have a positive effect on our mood. Get up ten minutes earlier than usual and then go about your day as usual: you'll see that everything will seem easier. It may not seem like much at first, but you'll find that those extra few minutes will make it possible for you to start off on the right foot, and you'll feel much more serene and at peace with yourself.

Do a
DIGITAL DETOX

By now, our lives are dominated by cell phones, emails, and social media. While it's true that we also use our smartphones as a means of entertainment, there's no doubt that we've become slaves to them, almost without realizing it. This addiction produces a stressful effect on us and is certainly not conducive to relaxation, enjoyment, or socialization. We're so immersed in the digital world that we find ourselves staring at our cell phones every minute, from the moment we wake up to the moment we go to sleep, even checking our email on holidays and weekends. This hyperconnectivity distracts us from important things, makes us less efficient, and never allows us to take a real break. There's no need to become a hermit and disconnect from the world completely, but there are small steps we can take to create new and healthy habits that will make us feel better and give us back some of our precious time.

DON'T EMAIL IN THE EVENING

Make sure you don't check your email again after a certain time in the evening: it won't be the end of the world if you answer an email the next morning.

If you can't follow this good practice every day, at least try to do so now and then; you will still reap the benefits.

TURN OFF YOUR TV AND CELL PHONE

Turn off all devices before going to sleep
and read a few pages of that book that's been lying on
your bedside table for longer than you can remember.

This is a fundamental step to sleeping well. In fact, the light emitted by TVs, PCs, and cell phones promotes insomnia, as it blocks the production of melatonin, the hormone that regulates sleep. Being addicted to electronic devices is not healthy. Get used to pulling the plug when you go to bed: read, learn to listen to your thoughts, or connect with the people around you.

TURN OFF NOTIFICATIONS

Turn off the "allow notifications" feature associated with your
email, calendar, and other applications:
if someone really needs you they can call you.

Notifications are a source of distraction that constantly interrupt our day and threaten to compromise our performance, both professionally and personally. Not only, but multitasking can easily make us feel overwhelmed. When too much information is coming at us, or we have too many tasks to attend to at once, we are prone to becoming anxious. This, in turn, causes us to lose focus and, in the end, we waste the time and energy we need to achieve our goals. So, turn off your notifications and make a list of priorities so you can focus on individual tasks without distractions.

STAY OFFLINE WHEN YOU WAKE UP

Commit yourself to not looking at your phone
until you get to work.
Instead, listen to music or talk to someone, or
take in the view of the people around you.

For most of us, by now, our first instinct when we wake up is to check our smartphone for updates to social media, the web, and/or our email inbox. This habit is not conducive to focusing on the present moment and can even have a negative impact on our mood if we happen to read bad news or negative comments. Because a healthy morning routine is essential for the success of your day, give yourself the gift of a peaceful breakfast, listen to your favorite music, relate to those around you, and stay offline until you get to work.

RECLAIM HUMAN RELATIONSHIPS

Instead of being glued to a screen all day,
try to engage in a genuine
conversation with someone.

The abuse of digital technology is threatening genuine human relationships and putting our cognitive functions at risk. Talk to real people, have a coffee with a colleague, call a friend, and get used to engaging your mind and your five senses for everyday activities.

Do a **DIGITAL DETOX**

24-HOUR DETOX

Try disabling your messaging and social media apps
and stop surfing the internet for a whole day.

Does it seem impossible? Try it out and you'll realize not only how easy it is, but also how much better you'll feel and how much more time you'll have to do things, talk to people, and focus on what you're doing. Spend time taking care of yourself, enjoy the outdoors, be mindful, and reclaim your ability to think, be curious about the world around you, and be creative.

OFFLINE ENTERTAINMENT

Whether in the gym, at a restaurant,
on a trip, or on a walk,
set your smartphone aside and
experience the present moment to the fullest.

Especially in times of high stress, it is common to spend a lot of time online, under the false impression that it will provide a good distraction. It has become so automatic for us to have our mobile in our hands, in fact, that we don't realize how dependent we are on them, even when we don't need them. Enjoy your free time offline, instead: in a restaurant, chat with people about real life situations. When you're exercising, focus exclusively on your movements and breathing and, if you're taking a walk or a trip out of town, listen to the sounds of nature, savor the aromas, and look about you.

TAKE CARE OF YOURSELF
and others

It's not often that we stop to take care of ourselves as we rush through our daily routines: we run out of the house and then return just as quickly because of all of the things we feel we have to do. We're always in such a rush that we don't even have time to look at ourselves in the mirror, let alone make eye contact with someone else who passes by. Change your attitude and try to listen; take care of yourself and be open to the needs of others: relationships are important, and every smile you bestow on someone will do wonders for your own mood..

ACCEPT WHO YOU ARE
Be kind to yourself: don't always blame yourself.
Take a three-minute break in front of the mirror
and learn to love what you see.

No one is perfect: everyone can make mistakes, and each of us has plenty of room for improvement. However, being hypercritical and too demanding, feeling guilty about your faults or failures, won't help you become a different person but will only undermine your self-esteem. Start loving what you see in the mirror and use it as a starting point to build the best version of yourself.

SMILE AT SOMEONE

Be kind to someone,
whether it be a colleague, a neighbor,
or a needy person along the street.

A smile costs us nothing, and yet it can be of surprising value for those who receive it. Too often we are so caught up in our own thoughts that we don't even notice those who pass by us, let alone those whom we see every day, or family members who, unbeknownst to us, may be struggling with a problem of their own. Open your eyes and your heart, and be gentle and helpful to others instead of just thinking about yourself. You'll experience a sense of fulfillment, and, more than likely, before long your worries will begin to seem futile to you.

A DOSE OF WELL-BEING

If you're feeling a bit down,
treat yourself to a restorative massage,
a session with a beautician,
or a good glass of wine.

Don't wait for a special occasion to treat yourself to something that makes you feel good. If you feel tired, try to give yourself some time to relax: go for a massage, a manicure, or set up a hairstyling appointment. Do you only have ten minutes? After work, meet up with a friend for a good glass of wine or stop by a pastry shop for a special treat: you're guaranteed to improve your mood!

TAKE CARE OF YOUR APPEARANCE

Wake up a little earlier than usual and
give yourself a little extra time to prepare for the day:
choose your outfit and accessories with care,
and pay attention to your grooming.

From time to time, set aside a little extra time to devote the attention you want to your appearance: select your clothes carefully, making sure fabrics and colors go well together, and wear accessories that you usually don't use because you're too rushed. Take particular care of your hair and skincare and don't forget to use sunscreen and moisturizing treatments.

AN EVENING OF RELAXATION

Try to reconnect with your biological clock
and follow your natural rhythms.

On the weekend, get organized to carve out a quiet, commitment-free evening, just for you. Put away all electronic devices, turn off the TV, and relax: read a good book, listen to your favorite music, or take a hot bath. Prepare a healthy and nutritious dinner, sip an herbal tea, and then go to sleep as soon as you feel sleepy, without looking at your cell phone or setting the alarm. At what time did you go to bed? How many hours did you sleep? Being aware of these things is a way of understanding how your biological clock would work if it wasn't subjected to imposed rhythms: you may not always be able do this, but once in a while it will do you a lot of good.

TAKE CARE OF YOURSELF and others

PAY ATTENTION TO OTHERS

Pay someone a sincere compliment;
ask them "How are you?"
and be prepared to help a person in need.

Don't forget that we derive happiness also in giving and taking care of others. No one can be happy who is solely caught up in him/herself. So, turn your gaze outward and give some loving and sincere attention to your friends, acquaintances, and anyone you run into.

CONTEMPLATE BEAUTY

Stop to take in a sunset,
go see an exhibition,
a good movie, or a theater show.

Slow down for a moment and stop to contemplate the beauty around you: this beauty may be in the form of a beautiful piece of art, the work of a painter or playwright, or it may be in the form of nature itself. No matter where you are, whether you're stuck in traffic or running around getting errands done, stop for a few minutes in a comfortable spot and enjoy the spectacle of the setting sun. Observe how the whole panorama is tinged with shades of pink, red, and yellow. Just a few moments like this will make you feel calmer and more relaxed, evoke a sensation of awe and wonder in you, and let you hit the reset button, so you can live in the present moment and recharge at the end of the day.

EMERGENCY SOLUTIONS
for off days

Some days we feel really low, whether it be because we are overtired, or something has saddened us, we're worried about something, or we just plain don't feel well, but we still have things we have to do. When this happens to you, try to go easy on yourself, and allow yourself some concessions: you don't always have to project the perfect, flawless you. It is OK to say you need some "me time", to feel like sulking or crying, or simply not to talk to anyone. Allow yourself to live through these dark moments as needed: it will permit you to let off steam and put things in perspective, so you can catch your breath and get ready to set off again on the right foot.

SEND AN S.O.S. OUT TO YOUR FRIENDS

Reach out to a friend for help:
even going out for a coffee together or
having a good chat over the phone will do the job.

When you can't stop seeing the negative in everything, ask for help from those who love you. Sometimes even just talking for a few minutes to someone with a friendly ear, so you can let off steam and get advice, can help you clear your head, work through a problem, and turn your day around.

THE ART OF TIDYING UP

Spend ten minutes tidying up your room,
hang up the clothes that you've left lying about
and get rid of the unnecessary paperwork on your desk.

When you feel like your life is out of control, one of the most effective ways to reel it back in is to focus on small, concrete steps you can take to hit the reset button and return to a state of equilibrium. One such way is by tidying up: putting things in order and cleaning are highly cathartic activities, because they clear the decks for unencumbered thought. When you tidy up, you free yourself from physical burdens, the first step to lightening your mental load and regaining control of yourself. This is all it takes to reposition you, so that you can find serenity and harmony.

IMMERSE YOURSELF IN NATURE!

Find a quiet place in the outdoors and listen:
try to distinguish at least three different sounds
and focus on how they make you feel.

Go into a park, in your garden, or wherever you can come into contact with nature: try to notice, beyond the cacophony of voices and passing cars, the sounds of nature, whether it be the chirping of birds or the rustling of the wind in the trees. Take a long walk or just sit somewhere for a few moments: you are bound to feel invigorated and more at peace after having done so.

EMERGENCY SOLUTIONS for off days

FIND YOUR COMFORT ZONE
Give in to a moment of comfort:
enjoy a hot drink from your favorite cup, or snuggle
under a warm blanket and watch a movie you love

If you've had a bad day, pamper yourself in the most spontaneous way you can think of. Allow yourself a treat and try to turn this moment into something special, even magical, like a child might do. Don't just drink hot chocolate, drink it from an elegant cup, maybe while under a soft and fluffy blanket, with a nice movie playing in the background.

PRIORITIZE YOURSELF
When you don't feel like it,
don't try to be perfect at all costs:
just do what you feel like doing.

If you feel too tired, too sad, or are lacking in energy, put yourself first for once without feeling guilty: cancel the dinner you didn't really want to go to, postpone the appointment with that pile of clothes that's been waiting to be ironed, don't force yourself to answer yet another phone call where you'll have to listen to someone else's problems. Go for a drive on your own, order take-out from your favorite comfort food restaurant, take a nap, or choose to do nothing until you feel like it, without being accountable to anyone. Let the world go on without you for a while.

EMERGENCY SOLUTIONS for off days

TAKE IT ONE DAY AT A TIME

Don't worry about tomorrow,
think about today.
Make a list of all the things you've got to do
and start by doing one of them.

There's no need to struggle to solve all your problems at once, but there's also no need to postpone the more tedious tasks that are making you feel anxious: make a list of them and tackle one thing at a time. You'll feel so much better!

LIVE IN THE MOMENT

Try practicing meditation:
even ten minutes a day
of focusing on the present moment
can help you overcome your worries.

When you're feeling suffocated by thoughts and commitments, don't just keep going on "autopilot" and don't let yourself be drawn into a whirlwind of anxiety. Stop and meditate for a few minutes (if you've never done it, look for a teacher and take a trial lesson): practice using your senses to reconnect with the "here and now", focusing only on the present. What sounds, images, and sensations do you perceive? What do you feel? Meditation is a good daily practice to achieve inner peace and be happier.

Happy the Man,
and happy he alone,
he who can call
TODAY
HIS OWN!
John Dryden

SU MO TU WE TH FR SA

GRATITUDE Today I am grateful for . . .

OBJECTIVES Today my priority is . . .

TIME FOR MYSELF Today I want to . . .

HAPPINESS A beautiful thing that happened today was . . .

SUCCESS An obstacle I overcame today was . . .

MEMO TO SELF I would have improved my day if . . .

GRATITUDE Today I am grateful for . . .

OBJECTIVES Today my priority is . . .

TIME FOR MYSELF Today I want to . . .

HAPPINESS A beautiful thing that happened today was . . .

SUCCESS An obstacle I overcame today was . . .

MEMO TO SELF I would have improved my day if . . .

SU MO TU WE TH FR SA

GRATITUDE Today I am grateful for . . .

OBJECTIVES Today my priority is . . .

TIME FOR MYSELF Today I want to . . .

HAPPINESS A beautiful thing that happened today was . . .

SUCCESS An obstacle I overcame today was . . .

MEMO TO SELF I would have improved my day if . . .

GRATITUDE Today I am grateful for . . .

OBJECTIVES Today my priority is . . .

TIME FOR MYSELF Today I want to . . .

HAPPINESS A beautiful thing that happened today was . . .

SUCCESS An obstacle I overcame today was . . .

MEMO TO SELF I would have improved my day if . . .

GRATITUDE Today I am grateful for . . .

OBJECTIVES Today my priority is . . .

TIME FOR MYSELF Today I want to . . .

HAPPINESS A beautiful thing that happened today was . . .

SUCCESS An obstacle I overcame today was . . .

MEMO TO SELF I would have improved my day if . . .

GRATITUDE Today I am grateful for . . .

OBJECTIVES Today my priority is . . .

TIME FOR MYSELF Today I want to . . .

HAPPINESS A beautiful thing that happened today was . . .

SUCCESS An obstacle I overcame today was . . .

MEMO TO SELF I would have improved my day if . . .

GRATITUDE Today I am grateful for . . .

OBJECTIVES Today my priority is . . .

TIME FOR MYSELF Today I want to . . .

HAPPINESS A beautiful thing that happened today was . . .

SUCCESS An obstacle I overcame today was . . .

MEMO TO SELF I would have improved my day if . . .

A JOURNEY
of a thousand Miles
BEGINS
with a
SINGLE STEP.
Lao Tzu

SU MO TU WE TH FR SA

GRATITUDE Today I am grateful for . . .

OBJECTIVES Today my priority is . . .

TIME FOR MYSELF Today I want to . . .

HAPPINESS A beautiful thing that happened today was . . .

SUCCESS An obstacle I overcame today was . . .

MEMO TO SELF I would have improved my day if . . .

SU MO TU WE TH FR SA

GRATITUDE Today I am grateful for . . .

OBJECTIVES Today my priority is . . .

TIME FOR MYSELF Today I want to . . .

HAPPINESS A beautiful thing that happened today was . . .

SUCCESS An obstacle I overcame today was . . .

MEMO TO SELF I would have improved my day if . . .

GRATITUDE Today I am grateful for . . .

OBJECTIVES Today my priority is . . .

TIME FOR MYSELF Today I want to . . .

HAPPINESS A beautiful thing that happened today was . . .

SUCCESS An obstacle I overcame today was . . .

MEMO TO SELF I would have improved my day if . . .

month

day

year

SU · MO · TU · WE · TH · FR · SA

GRATITUDE Today I am grateful for . . .

OBJECTIVES Today my priority is . . .

TIME FOR MYSELF Today I want to . . .

HAPPINESS A beautiful thing that happened today was . . .

SUCCESS An obstacle I overcame today was . . .

MEMO TO SELF I would have improved my day if . . .

GRATITUDE Today I am grateful for . . .

OBJECTIVES Today my priority is . . .

TIME FOR MYSELF Today I want to . . .

HAPPINESS A beautiful thing that happened today was . . .

SUCCESS An obstacle I overcame today was . . .

MEMO TO SELF I would have improved my day if . . .

GRATITUDE Today I am grateful for . . .

OBJECTIVES Today my priority is . . .

TIME FOR MYSELF Today I want to . . .

HAPPINESS A beautiful thing that happened today was . . .

SUCCESS An obstacle I overcame today was . . .

MEMO TO SELF I would have improved my day if . . .

GRATITUDE Today I am grateful for . . .

OBJECTIVES Today my priority is . . .

TIME FOR MYSELF Today I want to . . .

HAPPINESS A beautiful thing that happened today was . . .

SUCCESS An obstacle I overcame today was . . .

MEMO TO SELF I would have improved my day if . . .

Love of
BUSTLE
is not INDUSTRY—
it is only the
RESTLESSNESS
of a hunted mind.
Seneca

month

day

year

SU MO TU WE TH FR SA

GRATITUDE Today I am grateful for . . .

OBJECTIVES Today my priority is . . .

TIME FOR MYSELF Today I want to . . .

HAPPINESS A beautiful thing that happened today was . . .

SUCCESS An obstacle I overcame today was . . .

MEMO TO SELF I would have improved my day if . . .

GRATITUDE Today I am grateful for . . .

OBJECTIVES Today my priority is . . .

TIME FOR MYSELF Today I want to . . .

HAPPINESS A beautiful thing that happened today was . . .

SUCCESS An obstacle I overcame today was . . .

MEMO TO SELF I would have improved my day if . . .

GRATITUDE Today I am grateful for . . .

OBJECTIVES Today my priority is . . .

TIME FOR MYSELF Today I want to . . .

HAPPINESS A beautiful thing that happened today was . . .

SUCCESS An obstacle I overcame today was . . .

MEMO TO SELF I would have improved my day if . . .

SU MO TU WE TH FR SA

GRATITUDE Today I am grateful for . . .

OBJECTIVES Today my priority is . . .

TIME FOR MYSELF Today I want to . . .

HAPPINESS A beautiful thing that happened today was . . .

SUCCESS An obstacle I overcame today was . . .

MEMO TO SELF I would have improved my day if . . .

GRATITUDE Today I am grateful for . . .

OBJECTIVES Today my priority is . . .

TIME FOR MYSELF Today I want to . . .

HAPPINESS A beautiful thing that happened today was . . .

SUCCESS An obstacle I overcame today was . . .

MEMO TO SELF I would have improved my day if . . .

GRATITUDE Today I am grateful for . . .

OBJECTIVES Today my priority is . . .

TIME FOR MYSELF Today I want to . . .

HAPPINESS A beautiful thing that happened today was . . .

SUCCESS An obstacle I overcame today was . . .

MEMO TO SELF I would have improved my day if . . .

GRATITUDE Today I am grateful for . . .

OBJECTIVES Today my priority is . . .

TIME FOR MYSELF Today I want to . . .

HAPPINESS A beautiful thing that happened today was . . .

SUCCESS An obstacle I overcame today was . . .

MEMO TO SELF I would have improved my day if . . .

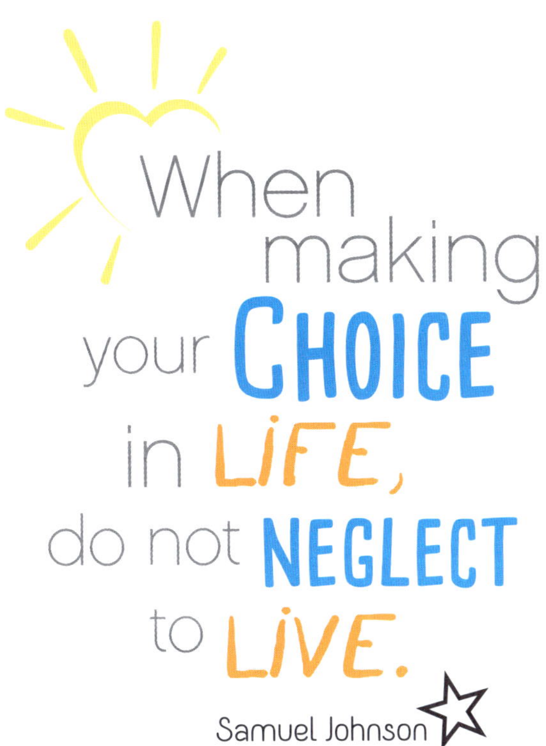

When making your CHOICE in LIFE, do not NEGLECT to LIVE.
Samuel Johnson

month   day   year

SU MO TU WE TH FR SA

GRATITUDE Today I am grateful for . . .

OBJECTIVES Today my priority is . . .

TIME FOR MYSELF Today I want to . . .

HAPPINESS A beautiful thing that happened today was . . .

SUCCESS An obstacle I overcame today was . . .

MEMO TO SELF I would have improved my day if . . .

SU MO TU WE TH FR SA

GRATITUDE Today I am grateful for . . .

OBJECTIVES Today my priority is . . .

TIME FOR MYSELF Today I want to . . .

HAPPINESS A beautiful thing that happened today was . . .

SUCCESS An obstacle I overcame today was . . .

MEMO TO SELF I would have improved my day if . . .

month
day
year

(SU) (MO) (TU) (WE) (TH) (FR) (SA)

GRATITUDE Today I am grateful for . . .

OBJECTIVES Today my priority is . . .

TIME FOR MYSELF Today I want to . . .

HAPPINESS A beautiful thing that happened today was . . .

SUCCESS An obstacle I overcame today was . . .

MEMO TO SELF I would have improved my day if . . .

SU MO TU WE TH FR SA

GRATITUDE Today I am grateful for . . .

OBJECTIVES Today my priority is . . .

TIME FOR MYSELF Today I want to . . .

HAPPINESS A beautiful thing that happened today was . . .

SUCCESS An obstacle I overcame today was . . .

MEMO TO SELF I would have improved my day if . . .

GRATITUDE Today I am grateful for . . .

OBJECTIVES Today my priority is . . .

TIME FOR MYSELF Today I want to . . .

HAPPINESS A beautiful thing that happened today was . . .

SUCCESS An obstacle I overcame today was . . .

MEMO TO SELF I would have improved my day if . . .

GRATITUDE Today I am grateful for . . .

OBJECTIVES Today my priority is . . .

TIME FOR MYSELF Today I want to . . .

HAPPINESS A beautiful thing that happened today was . . .

SUCCESS An obstacle I overcame today was . . .

MEMO TO SELF I would have improved my day if . . .

GRATITUDE Today I am grateful for . . .

OBJECTIVES Today my priority is . . .

TIME FOR MYSELF Today I want to . . .

HAPPINESS A beautiful thing that happened today was . . .

SUCCESS An obstacle I overcame today was . . .

MEMO TO SELF I would have improved my day if . . .

With the new
DAY comes
new STRENGTH
and new
THOUGHTS.
Eleanor Roosevelt

GRATITUDE Today I am grateful for . . .

OBJECTIVES Today my priority is . . .

TIME FOR MYSELF Today I want to . . .

HAPPINESS A beautiful thing that happened today was . . .

SUCCESS An obstacle I overcame today was . . .

MEMO TO SELF I would have improved my day if . . .

GRATITUDE Today I am grateful for . . .

OBJECTIVES Today my priority is . . .

TIME FOR MYSELF Today I want to . . .

HAPPINESS A beautiful thing that happened today was . . .

SUCCESS An obstacle I overcame today was . . .

MEMO TO SELF I would have improved my day if . . .

SU MO TU WE TH FR SA

GRATITUDE Today I am grateful for . . .

OBJECTIVES Today my priority is . . .

TIME FOR MYSELF Today I want to . . .

HAPPINESS A beautiful thing that happened today was . . .

SUCCESS An obstacle I overcame today was . . .

MEMO TO SELF I would have improved my day if . . .

GRATITUDE Today I am grateful for . . .

OBJECTIVES Today my priority is . . .

TIME FOR MYSELF Today I want to . . .

HAPPINESS A beautiful thing that happened today was . . .

SUCCESS An obstacle I overcame today was . . .

MEMO TO SELF I would have improved my day if . . .

SU MO TU WE TH FR SA

GRATITUDE Today I am grateful for . . .

OBJECTIVES Today my priority is . . .

TIME FOR MYSELF Today I want to . . .

HAPPINESS A beautiful thing that happened today was . . .

SUCCESS An obstacle I overcame today was . . .

MEMO TO SELF I would have improved my day if . . .

SU MO TU WE TH FR SA

GRATITUDE Today I am grateful for . . .

OBJECTIVES Today my priority is . . .

TIME FOR MYSELF Today I want to . . .

HAPPINESS A beautiful thing that happened today was . . .

SUCCESS An obstacle I overcame today was . . .

MEMO TO SELF I would have improved my day if . . .

GRATITUDE Today I am grateful for . . .

OBJECTIVES Today my priority is . . .

TIME FOR MYSELF Today I want to . . .

HAPPINESS A beautiful thing that happened today was . . .

SUCCESS An obstacle I overcame today was . . .

MEMO TO SELF I would have improved my day if . . .

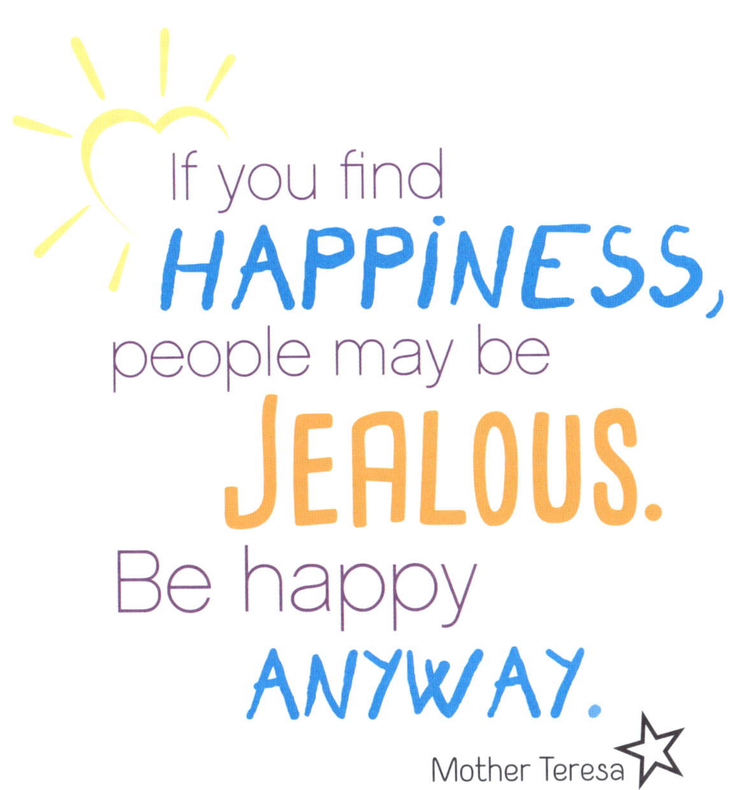

If you find
HAPPINESS,
people may be
JEALOUS.
Be happy
ANYWAY.
Mother Teresa

SU MO TU WE TH FR SA

GRATITUDE Today I am grateful for . . .

OBJECTIVES Today my priority is . . .

TIME FOR MYSELF Today I want to . . .

HAPPINESS A beautiful thing that happened today was . . .

SUCCESS An obstacle I overcame today was . . .

MEMO TO SELF I would have improved my day if . . .

GRATITUDE Today I am grateful for . . .

OBJECTIVES Today my priority is . . .

TIME FOR MYSELF Today I want to . . .

HAPPINESS A beautiful thing that happened today was . . .

SUCCESS An obstacle I overcame today was . . .

MEMO TO SELF I would have improved my day if . . .

SU MO TU WE TH FR SA

GRATITUDE Today I am grateful for . . .

OBJECTIVES Today my priority is . . .

TIME FOR MYSELF Today I want to . . .

HAPPINESS A beautiful thing that happened today was . . .

SUCCESS An obstacle I overcame today was . . .

MEMO TO SELF I would have improved my day if . . .

GRATITUDE Today I am grateful for . . .

OBJECTIVES Today my priority is . . .

TIME FOR MYSELF Today I want to . . .

HAPPINESS A beautiful thing that happened today was . . .

SUCCESS An obstacle I overcame today was . . .

MEMO TO SELF I would have improved my day if . . .

GRATITUDE Today I am grateful for . . .

OBJECTIVES Today my priority is . . .

TIME FOR MYSELF Today I want to . . .

HAPPINESS A beautiful thing that happened today was . . .

SUCCESS An obstacle I overcame today was . . .

MEMO TO SELF I would have improved my day if . . .

SU MO TU WE TH FR SA

GRATITUDE Today I am grateful for . . .

OBJECTIVES Today my priority is . . .

TIME FOR MYSELF Today I want to . . .

HAPPINESS A beautiful thing that happened today was . . .

SUCCESS An obstacle I overcame today was . . .

MEMO TO SELF I would have improved my day if . . .

SU MO TU WE TH FR SA

GRATITUDE Today I am grateful for . . .

OBJECTIVES Today my priority is . . .

TIME FOR MYSELF Today I want to . . .

HAPPINESS A beautiful thing that happened today was . . .

SUCCESS An obstacle I overcame today was . . .

MEMO TO SELF I would have improved my day if . . .

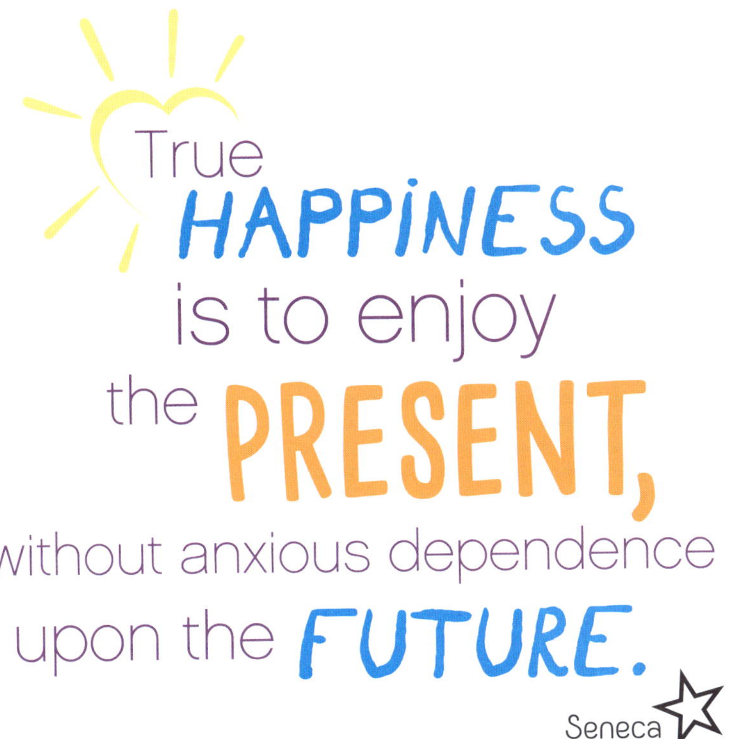

True
HAPPINESS
is to enjoy
the PRESENT,
without anxious dependence
upon the FUTURE.
Seneca

GRATITUDE Today I am grateful for . . .

OBJECTIVES Today my priority is . . .

TIME FOR MYSELF Today I want to . . .

HAPPINESS A beautiful thing that happened today was . . .

SUCCESS An obstacle I overcame today was . . .

MEMO TO SELF I would have improved my day if . . .

SU MO TU WE TH FR SA

GRATITUDE Today I am grateful for . . .

OBJECTIVES Today my priority is . . .

TIME FOR MYSELF Today I want to . . .

HAPPINESS A beautiful thing that happened today was . . .

SUCCESS An obstacle I overcame today was . . .

MEMO TO SELF I would have improved my day if . . .

GRATITUDE Today I am grateful for . . .

OBJECTIVES Today my priority is . . .

TIME FOR MYSELF Today I want to . . .

HAPPINESS A beautiful thing that happened today was . . .

SUCCESS An obstacle I overcame today was . . .

MEMO TO SELF I would have improved my day if . . .

GRATITUDE Today I am grateful for . . .

OBJECTIVES Today my priority is . . .

TIME FOR MYSELF Today I want to . . .

HAPPINESS A beautiful thing that happened today was . . .

SUCCESS An obstacle I overcame today was . . .

MEMO TO SELF I would have improved my day if . . .

GRATITUDE Today I am grateful for . . .

OBJECTIVES Today my priority is . . .

TIME FOR MYSELF Today I want to . . .

HAPPINESS A beautiful thing that happened today was . . .

SUCCESS An obstacle I overcame today was . . .

MEMO TO SELF I would have improved my day if . . .

SU MO TU WE TH FR SA

GRATITUDE Today I am grateful for . . .

OBJECTIVES Today my priority is . . .

TIME FOR MYSELF Today I want to . . .

HAPPINESS A beautiful thing that happened today was . . .

SUCCESS An obstacle I overcame today was . . .

MEMO TO SELF I would have improved my day if . . .

GRATITUDE Today I am grateful for . . .

OBJECTIVES Today my priority is . . .

TIME FOR MYSELF Today I want to . . .

HAPPINESS A beautiful thing that happened today was . . .

SUCCESS An obstacle I overcame today was . . .

MEMO TO SELF I would have improved my day if . . .

You must be the CHANGE you wish to SEE IN the WORLD.
Mahatma Gandhi

GRATITUDE Today I am grateful for . . .

OBJECTIVES Today my priority is . . .

TIME FOR MYSELF Today I want to . . .

HAPPINESS A beautiful thing that happened today was . . .

SUCCESS An obstacle I overcame today was . . .

MEMO TO SELF I would have improved my day if . . .

GRATITUDE Today I am grateful for . . .

OBJECTIVES Today my priority is . . .

TIME FOR MYSELF Today I want to . . .

HAPPINESS A beautiful thing that happened today was . . .

SUCCESS An obstacle I overcame today was . . .

MEMO TO SELF I would have improved my day if . . .

SU MO TU WE TH FR SA

GRATITUDE Today I am grateful for . . .

OBJECTIVES Today my priority is . . .

TIME FOR MYSELF Today I want to . . .

HAPPINESS A beautiful thing that happened today was . . .

SUCCESS An obstacle I overcame today was . . .

MEMO TO SELF I would have improved my day if . . .

SU MO TU WE TH FR SA

GRATITUDE Today I am grateful for . . .

OBJECTIVES Today my priority is . . .

TIME FOR MYSELF Today I want to . . .

HAPPINESS A beautiful thing that happened today was . . .

SUCCESS An obstacle I overcame today was . . .

MEMO TO SELF I would have improved my day if . . .

SU MO TU WE TH FR SA

GRATITUDE Today I am grateful for . . .

OBJECTIVES Today my priority is . . .

TIME FOR MYSELF Today I want to . . .

HAPPINESS A beautiful thing that happened today was . . .

SUCCESS An obstacle I overcame today was . . .

MEMO TO SELF I would have improved my day if . . .

SU MO TU WE TH FR SA

GRATITUDE Today I am grateful for . . .

OBJECTIVES Today my priority is . . .

TIME FOR MYSELF Today I want to . . .

HAPPINESS A beautiful thing that happened today was . . .

SUCCESS An obstacle I overcame today was . . .

MEMO TO SELF I would have improved my day if . . .

GRATITUDE Today I am grateful for . . .

OBJECTIVES Today my priority is . . .

TIME FOR MYSELF Today I want to . . .

HAPPINESS A beautiful thing that happened today was . . .

SUCCESS An obstacle I overcame today was . . .

MEMO TO SELF I would have improved my day if . . .

Remain in the MOMENT. Don't fall back into the PAST, and don't jump ahead to the FUTURE.
Osho

GRATITUDE Today I am grateful for . . .

OBJECTIVES Today my priority is . . .

TIME FOR MYSELF Today I want to . . .

HAPPINESS A beautiful thing that happened today was . . .

SUCCESS An obstacle I overcame today was . . .

MEMO TO SELF I would have improved my day if . . .

GRATITUDE Today I am grateful for . . .

OBJECTIVES Today my priority is . . .

TIME FOR MYSELF Today I want to . . .

HAPPINESS A beautiful thing that happened today was . . .

SUCCESS An obstacle I overcame today was . . .

MEMO TO SELF I would have improved my day if . . .

GRATITUDE Today I am grateful for . . .

OBJECTIVES Today my priority is . . .

TIME FOR MYSELF Today I want to . . .

HAPPINESS A beautiful thing that happened today was . . .

SUCCESS An obstacle I overcame today was . . .

MEMO TO SELF I would have improved my day if . . .

GRATITUDE Today I am grateful for . . .

OBJECTIVES Today my priority is . . .

TIME FOR MYSELF Today I want to . . .

HAPPINESS A beautiful thing that happened today was . . .

SUCCESS An obstacle I overcame today was . . .

MEMO TO SELF I would have improved my day if . . .

month   day   year

....

SU MO TU WE TH FR SA

GRATITUDE Today I am grateful for . . .

OBJECTIVES Today my priority is . . .

TIME FOR MYSELF Today I want to . . .

HAPPINESS A beautiful thing that happened today was . . .

SUCCESS An obstacle I overcame today was . . .

MEMO TO SELF I would have improved my day if . . .

month

day

year

SU MO TU WE TH FR SA

GRATITUDE Today I am grateful for . . .

OBJECTIVES Today my priority is . . .

TIME FOR MYSELF Today I want to . . .

HAPPINESS A beautiful thing that happened today was . . .

SUCCESS An obstacle I overcame today was . . .

MEMO TO SELF I would have improved my day if . . .

month day year

SU MO TU WE TH FR SA

GRATITUDE Today I am grateful for . . .

OBJECTIVES Today my priority is . . .

TIME FOR MYSELF Today I want to . . .

HAPPINESS A beautiful thing that happened today was . . .

SUCCESS An obstacle I overcame today was . . .

MEMO TO SELF I would have improved my day if . . .

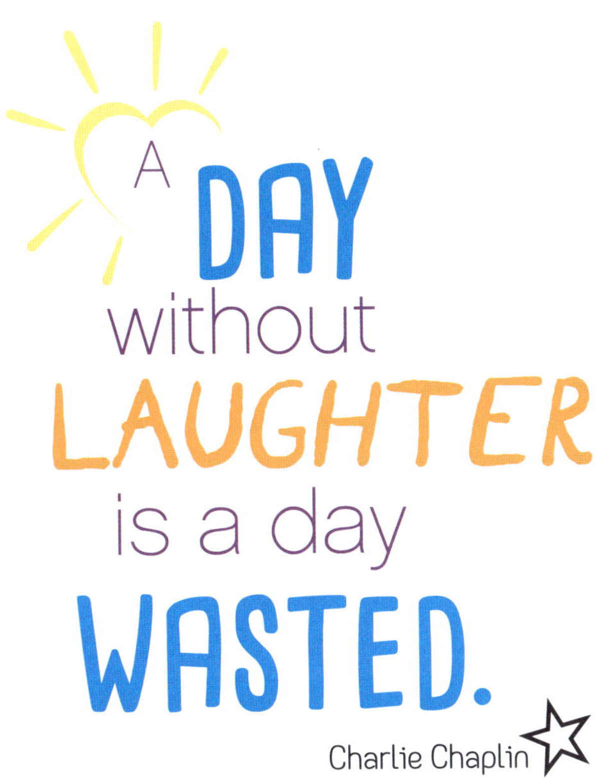

A
DAY
without
LAUGHTER
is a day
WASTED.
Charlie Chaplin

GRATITUDE Today I am grateful for . . .

OBJECTIVES Today my priority is . . .

TIME FOR MYSELF Today I want to . . .

HAPPINESS A beautiful thing that happened today was . . .

SUCCESS An obstacle I overcame today was . . .

MEMO TO SELF I would have improved my day if . . .

GRATITUDE Today I am grateful for . . .

OBJECTIVES Today my priority is . . .

TIME FOR MYSELF Today I want to . . .

HAPPINESS A beautiful thing that happened today was . . .

SUCCESS An obstacle I overcame today was . . .

MEMO TO SELF I would have improved my day if . . .

SU   MO   TU   WE   TH   FR   SA

GRATITUDE Today I am grateful for . . .

OBJECTIVES Today my priority is . . .

TIME FOR MYSELF Today I want to . . .

HAPPINESS A beautiful thing that happened today was . . .

SUCCESS An obstacle I overcame today was . . .

MEMO TO SELF I would have improved my day if . . .

GRATITUDE Today I am grateful for . . .

OBJECTIVES Today my priority is . . .

TIME FOR MYSELF Today I want to . . .

HAPPINESS A beautiful thing that happened today was . . .

SUCCESS An obstacle I overcame today was . . .

MEMO TO SELF I would have improved my day if . . .

GRATITUDE Today I am grateful for . . .

OBJECTIVES Today my priority is . . .

TIME FOR MYSELF Today I want to . . .

HAPPINESS A beautiful thing that happened today was . . .

SUCCESS An obstacle I overcame today was . . .

MEMO TO SELF I would have improved my day if . . .

month

day   year

....

....

SU MO WE TH SA
TU   FR

GRATITUDE Today I am grateful for . . .

OBJECTIVES Today my priority is . . .

TIME FOR MYSELF Today I want to . . .

HAPPINESS A beautiful thing that happened today was . . .

SUCCESS An obstacle I overcame today was . . .

MEMO TO SELF I would have improved my day if . . .

GRATITUDE Today I am grateful for . . .

OBJECTIVES Today my priority is . . .

TIME FOR MYSELF Today I want to . . .

HAPPINESS A beautiful thing that happened today was . . .

SUCCESS An obstacle I overcame today was . . .

MEMO TO SELF I would have improved my day if . . .

Small
OPPORTUNITIES
are often the beginning
of GREAT
ENTERPRISES.
Demosthenes

GRATITUDE Today I am grateful for . . .

OBJECTIVES Today my priority is . . .

TIME FOR MYSELF Today I want to . . .

HAPPINESS A beautiful thing that happened today was . . .

SUCCESS An obstacle I overcame today was . . .

MEMO TO SELF I would have improved my day if . . .

GRATITUDE Today I am grateful for . . .

OBJECTIVES Today my priority is . . .

TIME FOR MYSELF Today I want to . . .

HAPPINESS A beautiful thing that happened today was . . .

SUCCESS An obstacle I overcame today was . . .

MEMO TO SELF I would have improved my day if . . .

GRATITUDE Today I am grateful for . . .

OBJECTIVES Today my priority is . . .

TIME FOR MYSELF Today I want to . . .

HAPPINESS A beautiful thing that happened today was . . .

SUCCESS An obstacle I overcame today was . . .

MEMO TO SELF I would have improved my day if . . .

SU MO TU WE TH FR SA

GRATITUDE Today I am grateful for . . .

OBJECTIVES Today my priority is . . .

TIME FOR MYSELF Today I want to . . .

HAPPINESS A beautiful thing that happened today was . . .

SUCCESS An obstacle I overcame today was . . .

MEMO TO SELF I would have improved my day if . . .

GRATITUDE Today I am grateful for . . .

OBJECTIVES Today my priority is . . .

TIME FOR MYSELF Today I want to . . .

HAPPINESS A beautiful thing that happened today was . . .

SUCCESS An obstacle I overcame today was . . .

MEMO TO SELF I would have improved my day if . . .

SU MO TU WE TH FR SA

GRATITUDE Today I am grateful for . . .

OBJECTIVES Today my priority is . . .

TIME FOR MYSELF Today I want to . . .

HAPPINESS A beautiful thing that happened today was . . .

SUCCESS An obstacle I overcame today was . . .

MEMO TO SELF I would have improved my day if . . .

GRATITUDE Today I am grateful for . . .

OBJECTIVES Today my priority is . . .

TIME FOR MYSELF Today I want to . . .

HAPPINESS A beautiful thing that happened today was . . .

SUCCESS An obstacle I overcame today was . . .

MEMO TO SELF I would have improved my day if . . .

He who WISHES
to secure the good
of OTHERS
has already secured
HIS OWN.
Confucius

SU MO TU WE TH FR SA

GRATITUDE Today I am grateful for . . .

OBJECTIVES Today my priority is . . .

TIME FOR MYSELF Today I want to . . .

HAPPINESS A beautiful thing that happened today was . . .

SUCCESS An obstacle I overcame today was . . .

MEMO TO SELF I would have improved my day if . . .

SU MO TU WE TH FR SA

GRATITUDE Today I am grateful for . . .

OBJECTIVES Today my priority is . . .

TIME FOR MYSELF Today I want to . . .

HAPPINESS A beautiful thing that happened today was . . .

SUCCESS An obstacle I overcame today was . . .

MEMO TO SELF I would have improved my day if . . .

GRATITUDE Today I am grateful for . . .

OBJECTIVES Today my priority is . . .

TIME FOR MYSELF Today I want to . . .

HAPPINESS A beautiful thing that happened today was . . .

SUCCESS An obstacle I overcame today was . . .

MEMO TO SELF I would have improved my day if . . .

GRATITUDE Today I am grateful for . . .

OBJECTIVES Today my priority is . . .

TIME FOR MYSELF Today I want to . . .

HAPPINESS A beautiful thing that happened today was . . .

SUCCESS An obstacle I overcame today was . . .

MEMO TO SELF I would have improved my day if . . .

SU MO TU WE TH FR SA

GRATITUDE Today I am grateful for . . .

OBJECTIVES Today my priority is . . .

TIME FOR MYSELF Today I want to . . .

HAPPINESS A beautiful thing that happened today was . . .

SUCCESS An obstacle I overcame today was . . .

MEMO TO SELF I would have improved my day if . . .

GRATITUDE Today I am grateful for . . .

OBJECTIVES Today my priority is . . .

TIME FOR MYSELF Today I want to . . .

HAPPINESS A beautiful thing that happened today was . . .

SUCCESS An obstacle I overcame today was . . .

MEMO TO SELF I would have improved my day if . . .

GRATITUDE Today I am grateful for . . .

OBJECTIVES Today my priority is . . .

TIME FOR MYSELF Today I want to . . .

HAPPINESS A beautiful thing that happened today was . . .

SUCCESS An obstacle I overcame today was . . .

MEMO TO SELF I would have improved my day if . . .

One always has TIME enough, if one WILL apply it WELL.
Johann Wolfgang von Goethe

SU MO TU WE TH FR SA

GRATITUDE Today I am grateful for . . .

OBJECTIVES Today my priority is . . .

TIME FOR MYSELF Today I want to . . .

HAPPINESS A beautiful thing that happened today was . . .

SUCCESS An obstacle I overcame today was . . .

MEMO TO SELF I would have improved my day if . . .

GRATITUDE Today I am grateful for . . .

OBJECTIVES Today my priority is . . .

TIME FOR MYSELF Today I want to . . .

HAPPINESS A beautiful thing that happened today was . . .

SUCCESS An obstacle I overcame today was . . .

MEMO TO SELF I would have improved my day if . . .

GRATITUDE Today I am grateful for . . .

OBJECTIVES Today my priority is . . .

TIME FOR MYSELF Today I want to . . .

HAPPINESS A beautiful thing that happened today was . . .

SUCCESS An obstacle I overcame today was . . .

MEMO TO SELF I would have improved my day if . . .

SU MO TU WE TH FR SA

GRATITUDE Today I am grateful for . . .

OBJECTIVES Today my priority is . . .

TIME FOR MYSELF Today I want to . . .

HAPPINESS A beautiful thing that happened today was . . .

SUCCESS An obstacle I overcame today was . . .

MEMO TO SELF I would have improved my day if . . .

SU MO TU WE TH FR SA

GRATITUDE Today I am grateful for . . .

OBJECTIVES Today my priority is . . .

TIME FOR MYSELF Today I want to . . .

HAPPINESS A beautiful thing that happened today was . . .

SUCCESS An obstacle I overcame today was . . .

MEMO TO SELF I would have improved my day if . . .

SU   MO   TU   WE   TH   FR   SA

GRATITUDE Today I am grateful for . . .

OBJECTIVES Today my priority is . . .

TIME FOR MYSELF Today I want to . . .

HAPPINESS A beautiful thing that happened today was . . .

SUCCESS An obstacle I overcame today was . . .

MEMO TO SELF I would have improved my day if . . .

SU MO TU WE TH FR SA

GRATITUDE Today I am grateful for . . .

OBJECTIVES Today my priority is . . .

TIME FOR MYSELF Today I want to . . .

HAPPINESS A beautiful thing that happened today was . . .

SUCCESS An obstacle I overcame today was . . .

MEMO TO SELF I would have improved my day if . . .

For every MINUTE you are ANGRY you lose SIXTY SECONDS of HAPPINESS.
Ralph Waldo Emerson

GRATITUDE Today I am grateful for . . .

OBJECTIVES Today my priority is . . .

TIME FOR MYSELF Today I want to . . .

HAPPINESS A beautiful thing that happened today was . . .

SUCCESS An obstacle I overcame today was . . .

MEMO TO SELF I would have improved my day if . . .

SU　MO　TU　WE　TH　FR　SA

GRATITUDE Today I am grateful for . . .

OBJECTIVES Today my priority is . . .

TIME FOR MYSELF Today I want to . . .

HAPPINESS A beautiful thing that happened today was . . .

SUCCESS An obstacle I overcame today was . . .

MEMO TO SELF I would have improved my day if . . .

GRATITUDE Today I am grateful for . . .

OBJECTIVES Today my priority is . . .

TIME FOR MYSELF Today I want to . . .

HAPPINESS A beautiful thing that happened today was . . .

SUCCESS An obstacle I overcame today was . . .

MEMO TO SELF I would have improved my day if . . .

SU   MO   TU   WE   TH   FR   SA

GRATITUDE Today I am grateful for . . .

OBJECTIVES Today my priority is . . .

TIME FOR MYSELF Today I want to . . .

HAPPINESS A beautiful thing that happened today was . . .

SUCCESS An obstacle I overcame today was . . .

MEMO TO SELF I would have improved my day if . . .

GRATITUDE Today I am grateful for . . .

OBJECTIVES Today my priority is . . .

TIME FOR MYSELF Today I want to . . .

HAPPINESS A beautiful thing that happened today was . . .

SUCCESS An obstacle I overcame today was . . .

MEMO TO SELF I would have improved my day if . . .

month   day   year

SU MO TU WE TH FR SA

GRATITUDE Today I am grateful for . . .

OBJECTIVES Today my priority is . . .

TIME FOR MYSELF Today I want to . . .

HAPPINESS A beautiful thing that happened today was . . .

SUCCESS An obstacle I overcame today was . . .

MEMO TO SELF I would have improved my day if . . .

GRATITUDE Today I am grateful for . . .

OBJECTIVES Today my priority is . . .

TIME FOR MYSELF Today I want to . . .

HAPPINESS A beautiful thing that happened today was . . .

SUCCESS An obstacle I overcame today was . . .

MEMO TO SELF I would have improved my day if . . .

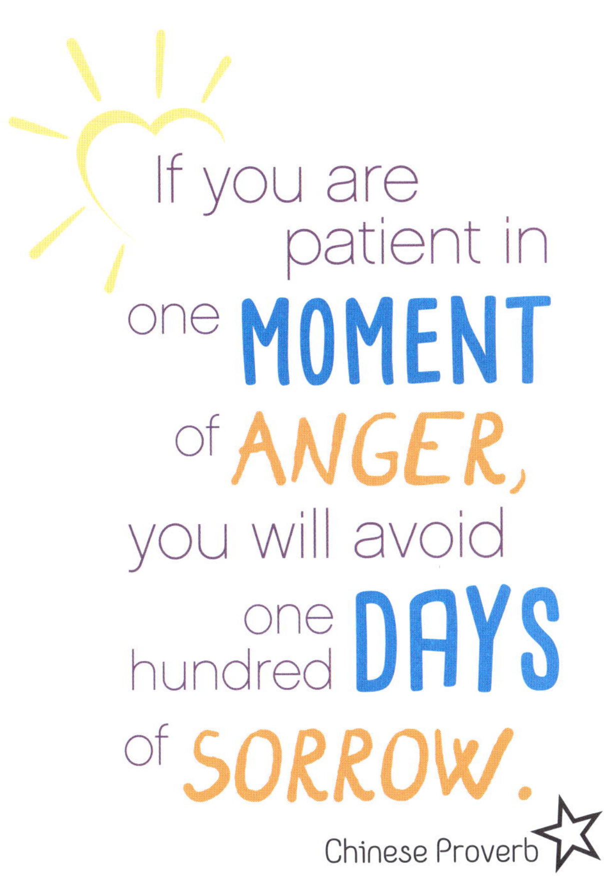
If you are
patient in
one MOMENT
of ANGER,
you will avoid
one DAYS
hundred
of SORROW.
Chinese Proverb

SU MO TU WE TH FR SA

GRATITUDE Today I am grateful for . . .

OBJECTIVES Today my priority is . . .

TIME FOR MYSELF Today I want to . . .

HAPPINESS A beautiful thing that happened today was . . .

SUCCESS An obstacle I overcame today was . . .

MEMO TO SELF I would have improved my day if . . .

GRATITUDE Today I am grateful for . . .

OBJECTIVES Today my priority is . . .

TIME FOR MYSELF Today I want to . . .

HAPPINESS A beautiful thing that happened today was . . .

SUCCESS An obstacle I overcame today was . . .

MEMO TO SELF I would have improved my day if . . .

SU MO TU WE TH FR SA

GRATITUDE Today I am grateful for . . .

OBJECTIVES Today my priority is . . .

TIME FOR MYSELF Today I want to . . .

HAPPINESS A beautiful thing that happened today was . . .

SUCCESS An obstacle I overcame today was . . .

MEMO TO SELF I would have improved my day if . . .

GRATITUDE Today I am grateful for . . .

OBJECTIVES Today my priority is . . .

TIME FOR MYSELF Today I want to . . .

HAPPINESS A beautiful thing that happened today was . . .

SUCCESS An obstacle I overcame today was . . .

MEMO TO SELF I would have improved my day if . . .

month   day   year

SU   MO   TU   WE   TH   FR   SA

GRATITUDE Today I am grateful for . . .

OBJECTIVES Today my priority is . . .

TIME FOR MYSELF Today I want to . . .

HAPPINESS A beautiful thing that happened today was . . .

SUCCESS An obstacle I overcame today was . . .

MEMO TO SELF I would have improved my day if . . .

SU MO TU WE TH FR SA

GRATITUDE Today I am grateful for . . .

OBJECTIVES Today my priority is . . .

TIME FOR MYSELF Today I want to . . .

HAPPINESS A beautiful thing that happened today was . . .

SUCCESS An obstacle I overcame today was . . .

MEMO TO SELF I would have improved my day if . . .

SU MO TU WE TH FR SA

GRATITUDE Today I am grateful for . . .

OBJECTIVES Today my priority is . . .

TIME FOR MYSELF Today I want to . . .

HAPPINESS A beautiful thing that happened today was . . .

SUCCESS An obstacle I overcame today was . . .

MEMO TO SELF I would have improved my day if . . .

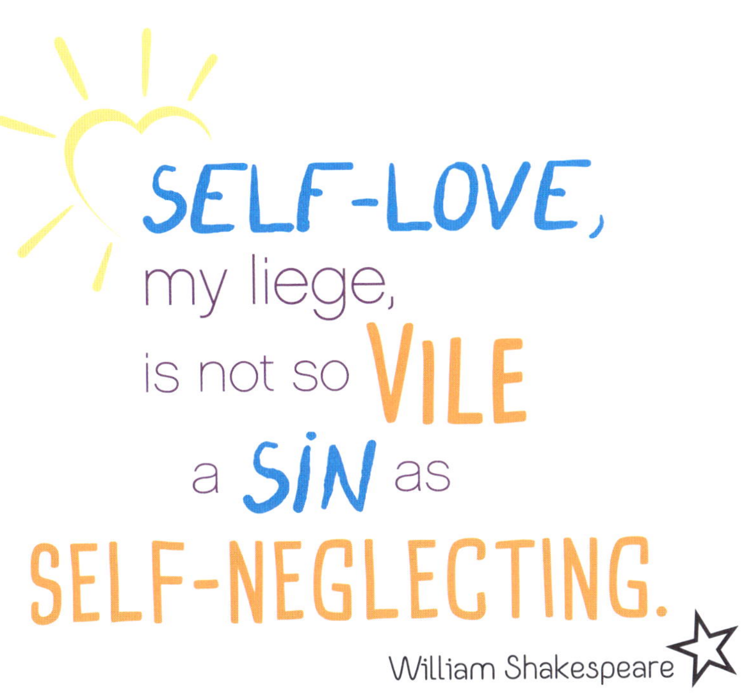
SELF-LOVE,
my liege,
is not so VILE
a SIN as
SELF-NEGLECTING.
William Shakespeare

GRATITUDE Today I am grateful for . . .

OBJECTIVES Today my priority is . . .

TIME FOR MYSELF Today I want to . . .

HAPPINESS A beautiful thing that happened today was . . .

SUCCESS An obstacle I overcame today was . . .

MEMO TO SELF I would have improved my day if . . .

GRATITUDE Today I am grateful for . . .

OBJECTIVES Today my priority is . . .

TIME FOR MYSELF Today I want to . . .

HAPPINESS A beautiful thing that happened today was . . .

SUCCESS An obstacle I overcame today was . . .

MEMO TO SELF I would have improved my day if . . .

GRATITUDE Today I am grateful for . . .

OBJECTIVES Today my priority is . . .

TIME FOR MYSELF Today I want to . . .

HAPPINESS A beautiful thing that happened today was . . .

SUCCESS An obstacle I overcame today was . . .

MEMO TO SELF I would have improved my day if . . .

GRATITUDE Today I am grateful for . . .

OBJECTIVES Today my priority is . . .

TIME FOR MYSELF Today I want to . . .

HAPPINESS A beautiful thing that happened today was . . .

SUCCESS An obstacle I overcame today was . . .

MEMO TO SELF I would have improved my day if . . .

GRATITUDE Today I am grateful for . . .

OBJECTIVES Today my priority is . . .

TIME FOR MYSELF Today I want to . . .

HAPPINESS A beautiful thing that happened today was . . .

SUCCESS An obstacle I overcame today was . . .

MEMO TO SELF I would have improved my day if . . .

month

day

year

SU MO TU WE TH FR SA

GRATITUDE Today I am grateful for . . .

OBJECTIVES Today my priority is . . .

TIME FOR MYSELF Today I want to . . .

HAPPINESS A beautiful thing that happened today was . . .

SUCCESS An obstacle I overcame today was . . .

MEMO TO SELF I would have improved my day if . . .

SU MO TU WE TH FR SA

GRATITUDE Today I am grateful for . . .

OBJECTIVES Today my priority is . . .

TIME FOR MYSELF Today I want to . . .

HAPPINESS A beautiful thing that happened today was . . .

SUCCESS An obstacle I overcame today was . . .

MEMO TO SELF I would have improved my day if . . .

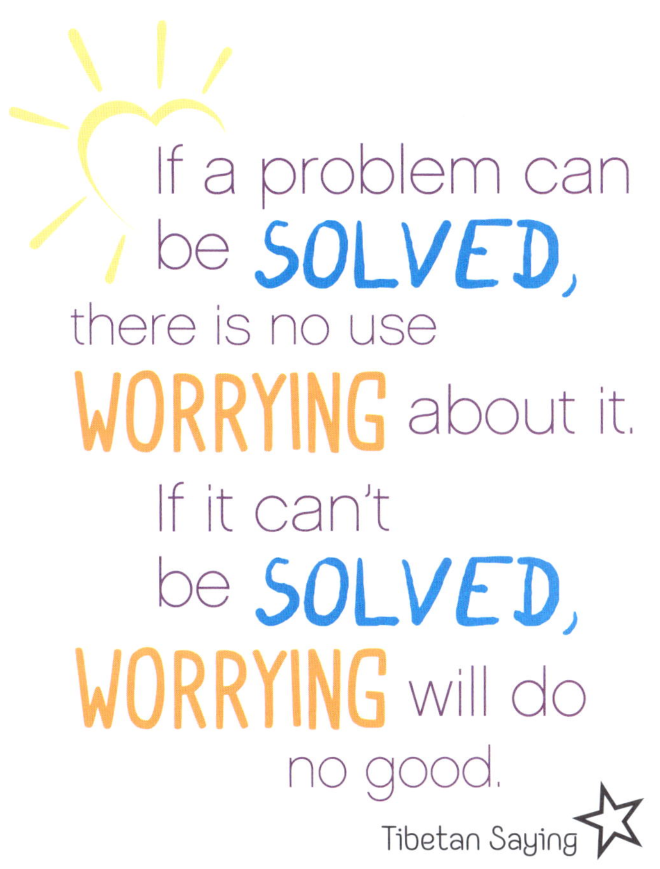

If a problem can be SOLVED, there is no use WORRYING about it.
If it can't be SOLVED, WORRYING will do no good.
Tibetan Saying

SU MO TU WE TH FR SA

GRATITUDE Today I am grateful for . . .

OBJECTIVES Today my priority is . . .

TIME FOR MYSELF Today I want to . . .

HAPPINESS A beautiful thing that happened today was . . .

SUCCESS An obstacle I overcame today was . . .

MEMO TO SELF I would have improved my day if . . .

SU MO TU WE TH FR SA

GRATITUDE Today I am grateful for . . .

OBJECTIVES Today my priority is . . .

TIME FOR MYSELF Today I want to . . .

HAPPINESS A beautiful thing that happened today was . . .

SUCCESS An obstacle I overcame today was . . .

MEMO TO SELF I would have improved my day if . . .

SU MO TU WE TH FR SA

GRATITUDE Today I am grateful for . . .

OBJECTIVES Today my priority is . . .

TIME FOR MYSELF Today I want to . . .

HAPPINESS A beautiful thing that happened today was . . .

SUCCESS An obstacle I overcame today was . . .

MEMO TO SELF I would have improved my day if . . .

SU MO TU WE TH FR SA

GRATITUDE Today I am grateful for . . .

OBJECTIVES Today my priority is . . .

TIME FOR MYSELF Today I want to . . .

HAPPINESS A beautiful thing that happened today was . . .

SUCCESS An obstacle I overcame today was . . .

MEMO TO SELF I would have improved my day if . . .

GRATITUDE Today I am grateful for . . .

OBJECTIVES Today my priority is . . .

TIME FOR MYSELF Today I want to . . .

HAPPINESS A beautiful thing that happened today was . . .

SUCCESS An obstacle I overcame today was . . .

MEMO TO SELF I would have improved my day if . . .

GRATITUDE Today I am grateful for . . .

OBJECTIVES Today my priority is . . .

TIME FOR MYSELF Today I want to . . .

HAPPINESS A beautiful thing that happened today was . . .

SUCCESS An obstacle I overcame today was . . .

MEMO TO SELF I would have improved my day if . . .

GRATITUDE Today I am grateful for . . .

OBJECTIVES Today my priority is . . .

TIME FOR MYSELF Today I want to . . .

HAPPINESS A beautiful thing that happened today was . . .

SUCCESS An obstacle I overcame today was . . .

MEMO TO SELF I would have improved my day if . . .

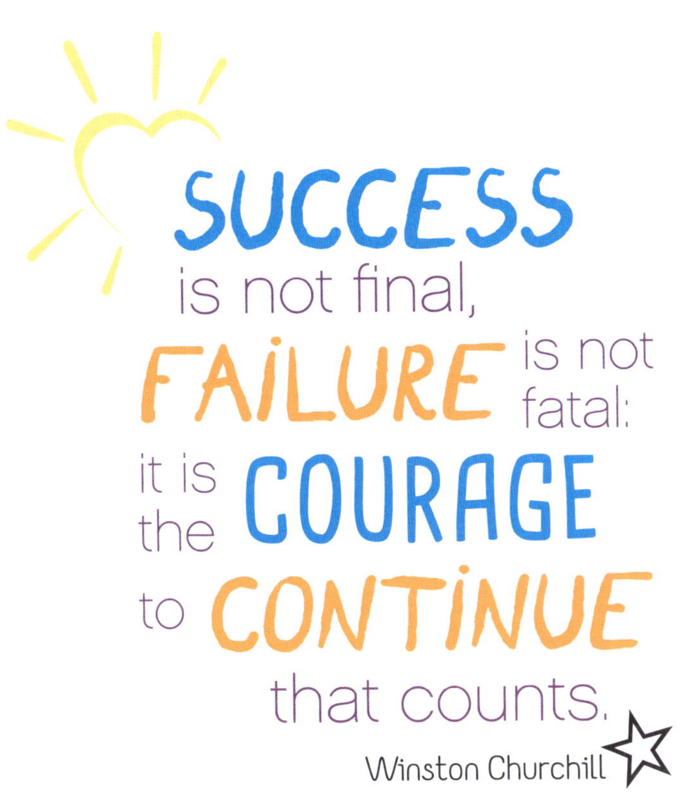

SUCCESS
is not final,
FAILURE is not fatal:
it is the COURAGE
to CONTINUE
that counts.
Winston Churchill

SU MO TU WE TH FR SA

GRATITUDE Today I am grateful for . . .

OBJECTIVES Today my priority is . . .

TIME FOR MYSELF Today I want to . . .

HAPPINESS A beautiful thing that happened today was . . .

SUCCESS An obstacle I overcame today was . . .

MEMO TO SELF I would have improved my day if . . .

GRATITUDE Today I am grateful for . . .

OBJECTIVES Today my priority is . . .

TIME FOR MYSELF Today I want to . . .

HAPPINESS A beautiful thing that happened today was . . .

SUCCESS An obstacle I overcame today was . . .

MEMO TO SELF I would have improved my day if . . .

GRATITUDE Today I am grateful for . . .

OBJECTIVES Today my priority is . . .

TIME FOR MYSELF Today I want to . . .

HAPPINESS A beautiful thing that happened today was . . .

SUCCESS An obstacle I overcame today was . . .

MEMO TO SELF I would have improved my day if . . .

GRATITUDE Today I am grateful for . . .

OBJECTIVES Today my priority is . . .

TIME FOR MYSELF Today I want to . . .

HAPPINESS A beautiful thing that happened today was . . .

SUCCESS An obstacle I overcame today was . . .

MEMO TO SELF I would have improved my day if . . .

SU MO TU WE TH FR SA

GRATITUDE Today I am grateful for . . .

OBJECTIVES Today my priority is . . .

TIME FOR MYSELF Today I want to . . .

HAPPINESS A beautiful thing that happened today was . . .

SUCCESS An obstacle I overcame today was . . .

MEMO TO SELF I would have improved my day if . . .

month

day

year

SU MO TU WE TH FR SA

GRATITUDE Today I am grateful for . . .

OBJECTIVES Today my priority is . . .

TIME FOR MYSELF Today I want to . . .

HAPPINESS A beautiful thing that happened today was . . .

SUCCESS An obstacle I overcame today was . . .

MEMO TO SELF I would have improved my day if . . .

GRATITUDE Today I am grateful for . . .

OBJECTIVES Today my priority is . . .

TIME FOR MYSELF Today I want to . . .

HAPPINESS A beautiful thing that happened today was . . .

SUCCESS An obstacle I overcame today was . . .

MEMO TO SELF I would have improved my day if . . .

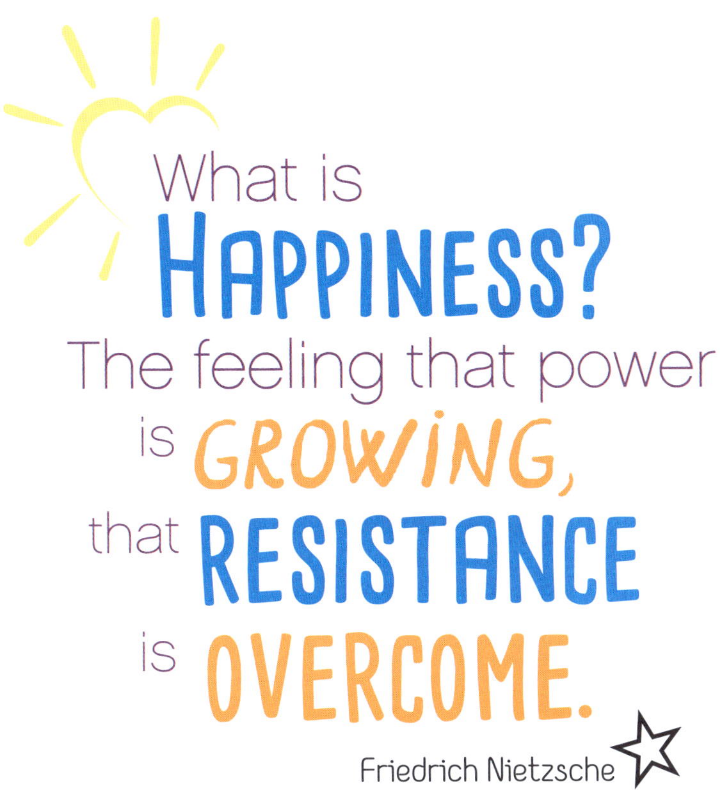

What is
HAPPINESS?
The feeling that power
is GROWING,
that RESISTANCE
is OVERCOME.
Friedrich Nietzsche

GRATITUDE Today I am grateful for . . .

OBJECTIVES Today my priority is . . .

TIME FOR MYSELF Today I want to . . .

HAPPINESS A beautiful thing that happened today was . . .

SUCCESS An obstacle I overcame today was . . .

MEMO TO SELF I would have improved my day if . . .

SU MO TU WE TH FR SA

GRATITUDE Today I am grateful for . . .

OBJECTIVES Today my priority is . . .

TIME FOR MYSELF Today I want to . . .

HAPPINESS A beautiful thing that happened today was . . .

SUCCESS An obstacle I overcame today was . . .

MEMO TO SELF I would have improved my day if . . .

GRATITUDE Today I am grateful for . . .

OBJECTIVES Today my priority is . . .

TIME FOR MYSELF Today I want to . . .

HAPPINESS A beautiful thing that happened today was . . .

SUCCESS An obstacle I overcame today was . . .

MEMO TO SELF I would have improved my day if . . .

GRATITUDE Today I am grateful for . . .

OBJECTIVES Today my priority is . . .

TIME FOR MYSELF Today I want to . . .

HAPPINESS A beautiful thing that happened today was . . .

SUCCESS An obstacle I overcame today was . . .

MEMO TO SELF I would have improved my day if . . .

GRATITUDE Today I am grateful for . . .

OBJECTIVES Today my priority is . . .

TIME FOR MYSELF Today I want to . . .

HAPPINESS A beautiful thing that happened today was . . .

SUCCESS An obstacle I overcame today was . . .

MEMO TO SELF I would have improved my day if . . .

GRATITUDE Today I am grateful for . . .

OBJECTIVES Today my priority is . . .

TIME FOR MYSELF Today I want to . . .

HAPPINESS A beautiful thing that happened today was . . .

SUCCESS An obstacle I overcame today was . . .

MEMO TO SELF I would have improved my day if . . .

GRATITUDE Today I am grateful for . . .

OBJECTIVES Today my priority is . . .

TIME FOR MYSELF Today I want to . . .

HAPPINESS A beautiful thing that happened today was . . .

SUCCESS An obstacle I overcame today was . . .

MEMO TO SELF I would have improved my day if . . .

It takes
COURAGE
to be
HAPPY.
Martha Woodroof

SU MO TU WE TH FR SA

GRATITUDE Today I am grateful for . . .

OBJECTIVES Today my priority is . . .

TIME FOR MYSELF Today I want to . . .

HAPPINESS A beautiful thing that happened today was . . .

SUCCESS An obstacle I overcame today was . . .

MEMO TO SELF I would have improved my day if . . .

GRATITUDE Today I am grateful for . . .

OBJECTIVES Today my priority is . . .

TIME FOR MYSELF Today I want to . . .

HAPPINESS A beautiful thing that happened today was . . .

SUCCESS An obstacle I overcame today was . . .

MEMO TO SELF I would have improved my day if . . .

SU MO TU WE TH FR SA

GRATITUDE Today I am grateful for . . .

OBJECTIVES Today my priority is . . .

TIME FOR MYSELF Today I want to . . .

HAPPINESS A beautiful thing that happened today was . . .

SUCCESS An obstacle I overcame today was . . .

MEMO TO SELF I would have improved my day if . . .

GRATITUDE Today I am grateful for . . .

OBJECTIVES Today my priority is . . .

TIME FOR MYSELF Today I want to . . .

HAPPINESS A beautiful thing that happened today was . . .

SUCCESS An obstacle I overcame today was . . .

MEMO TO SELF I would have improved my day if . . .

SU   MO   TU   WE   TH   FR   SA

GRATITUDE Today I am grateful for . . .

OBJECTIVES Today my priority is . . .

TIME FOR MYSELF Today I want to . . .

HAPPINESS A beautiful thing that happened today was . . .

SUCCESS An obstacle I overcame today was . . .

MEMO TO SELF I would have improved my day if . . .

GRATITUDE Today I am grateful for . . .

OBJECTIVES Today my priority is . . .

TIME FOR MYSELF Today I want to . . .

HAPPINESS A beautiful thing that happened today was . . .

SUCCESS An obstacle I overcame today was . . .

MEMO TO SELF I would have improved my day if . . .

SU MO TU WE TH FR SA

GRATITUDE Today I am grateful for . . .

OBJECTIVES Today my priority is . . .

TIME FOR MYSELF Today I want to . . .

HAPPINESS A beautiful thing that happened today was . . .

SUCCESS An obstacle I overcame today was . . .

MEMO TO SELF I would have improved my day if . . .

Where there
is LOVE,
there is NO
DARKNESS.
African Proverb

SU MO TU WE TH FR SA

GRATITUDE Today I am grateful for . . .

OBJECTIVES Today my priority is . . .

TIME FOR MYSELF Today I want to . . .

HAPPINESS A beautiful thing that happened today was . . .

SUCCESS An obstacle I overcame today was . . .

MEMO TO SELF I would have improved my day if . . .

GRATITUDE Today I am grateful for . . .

OBJECTIVES Today my priority is . . .

TIME FOR MYSELF Today I want to . . .

HAPPINESS A beautiful thing that happened today was . . .

SUCCESS An obstacle I overcame today was . . .

MEMO TO SELF I would have improved my day if . . .

GRATITUDE Today I am grateful for . . .

OBJECTIVES Today my priority is . . .

TIME FOR MYSELF Today I want to . . .

HAPPINESS A beautiful thing that happened today was . . .

SUCCESS An obstacle I overcame today was . . .

MEMO TO SELF I would have improved my day if . . .

GRATITUDE Today I am grateful for . . .

OBJECTIVES Today my priority is . . .

TIME FOR MYSELF Today I want to . . .

HAPPINESS A beautiful thing that happened today was . . .

SUCCESS An obstacle I overcame today was . . .

MEMO TO SELF I would have improved my day if . . .

GRATITUDE Today I am grateful for . . .

OBJECTIVES Today my priority is . . .

TIME FOR MYSELF Today I want to . . .

HAPPINESS A beautiful thing that happened today was . . .

SUCCESS An obstacle I overcame today was . . .

MEMO TO SELF I would have improved my day if . . .

GRATITUDE Today I am grateful for . . .

OBJECTIVES Today my priority is . . .

TIME FOR MYSELF Today I want to . . .

HAPPINESS A beautiful thing that happened today was . . .

SUCCESS An obstacle I overcame today was . . .

MEMO TO SELF I would have improved my day if . . .

GRATITUDE Today I am grateful for . . .

OBJECTIVES Today my priority is . . .

TIME FOR MYSELF Today I want to . . .

HAPPINESS A beautiful thing that happened today was . . .

SUCCESS An obstacle I overcame today was . . .

MEMO TO SELF I would have improved my day if . . .

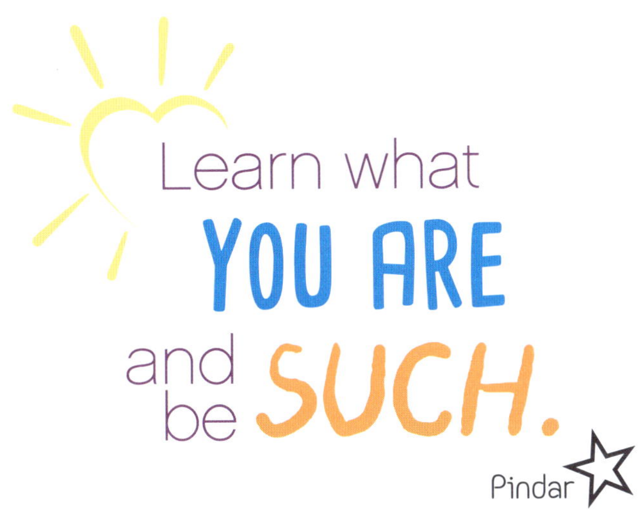

Learn what
YOU ARE
and
be SUCH.
Pindar

SU MO TU WE TH FR SA

GRATITUDE Today I am grateful for . . .

OBJECTIVES Today my priority is . . .

TIME FOR MYSELF Today I want to . . .

HAPPINESS A beautiful thing that happened today was . . .

SUCCESS An obstacle I overcame today was . . .

MEMO TO SELF I would have improved my day if . . .

SU MO TU WE TH FR SA

GRATITUDE Today I am grateful for . . .

OBJECTIVES Today my priority is . . .

TIME FOR MYSELF Today I want to . . .

HAPPINESS A beautiful thing that happened today was . . .

SUCCESS An obstacle I overcame today was . . .

MEMO TO SELF I would have improved my day if . . .

GRATITUDE Today I am grateful for . . .

OBJECTIVES Today my priority is . . .

TIME FOR MYSELF Today I want to . . .

HAPPINESS A beautiful thing that happened today was . . .

SUCCESS An obstacle I overcame today was . . .

MEMO TO SELF I would have improved my day if . . .

SU MO TU WE TH FR SA

GRATITUDE Today I am grateful for . . .

OBJECTIVES Today my priority is . . .

TIME FOR MYSELF Today I want to . . .

HAPPINESS A beautiful thing that happened today was . . .

SUCCESS An obstacle I overcame today was . . .

MEMO TO SELF I would have improved my day if . . .

GRATITUDE Today I am grateful for . . .

OBJECTIVES Today my priority is . . .

TIME FOR MYSELF Today I want to . . .

HAPPINESS A beautiful thing that happened today was . . .

SUCCESS An obstacle I overcame today was . . .

MEMO TO SELF I would have improved my day if . . .

GRATITUDE Today I am grateful for . . .

OBJECTIVES Today my priority is . . .

TIME FOR MYSELF Today I want to . . .

HAPPINESS A beautiful thing that happened today was . . .

SUCCESS An obstacle I overcame today was . . .

MEMO TO SELF I would have improved my day if . . .

GRATITUDE Today I am grateful for . . .

OBJECTIVES Today my priority is . . .

TIME FOR MYSELF Today I want to . . .

HAPPINESS A beautiful thing that happened today was . . .

SUCCESS An obstacle I overcame today was . . .

MEMO TO SELF I would have improved my day if . . .

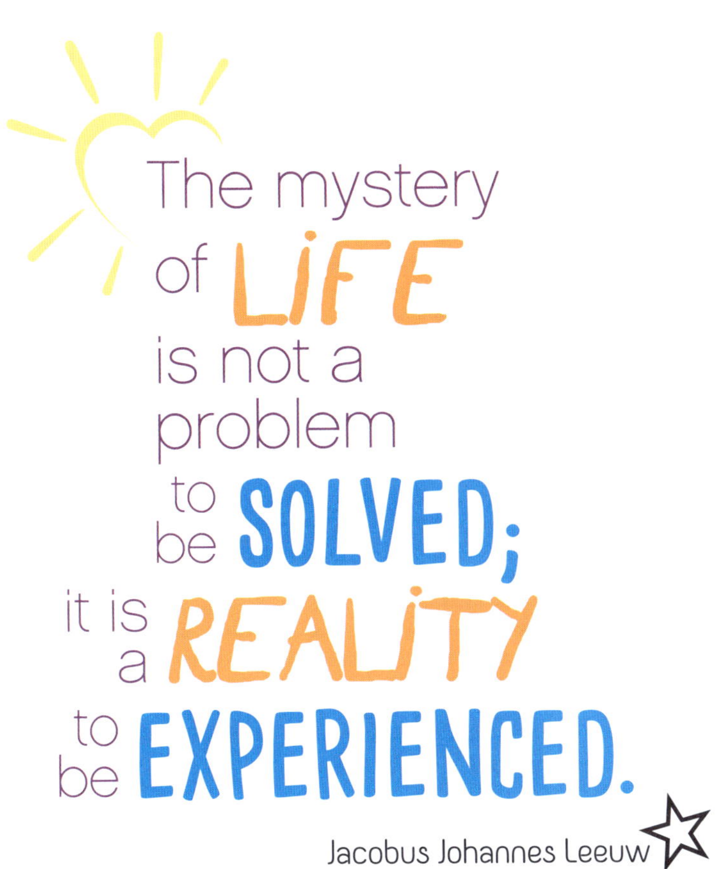

The mystery
of LIFE
is not a
problem
to be SOLVED;
it is a REALITY
to be EXPERIENCED.
Jacobus Johannes Leeuw

GRATITUDE Today I am grateful for . . .

OBJECTIVES Today my priority is . . .

TIME FOR MYSELF Today I want to . . .

HAPPINESS A beautiful thing that happened today was . . .

SUCCESS An obstacle I overcame today was . . .

MEMO TO SELF I would have improved my day if . . .

GRATITUDE Today I am grateful for . . .

OBJECTIVES Today my priority is . . .

TIME FOR MYSELF Today I want to . . .

HAPPINESS A beautiful thing that happened today was . . .

SUCCESS An obstacle I overcame today was . . .

MEMO TO SELF I would have improved my day if . . .

SU MO TU WE TH FR SA

GRATITUDE Today I am grateful for . . .

OBJECTIVES Today my priority is . . .

TIME FOR MYSELF Today I want to . . .

HAPPINESS A beautiful thing that happened today was . . .

SUCCESS An obstacle I overcame today was . . .

MEMO TO SELF I would have improved my day if . . .

SU MO TU WE TH FR SA

GRATITUDE Today I am grateful for . . .

OBJECTIVES Today my priority is . . .

TIME FOR MYSELF Today I want to . . .

HAPPINESS A beautiful thing that happened today was . . .

SUCCESS An obstacle I overcame today was . . .

MEMO TO SELF I would have improved my day if . . .

GRATITUDE Today I am grateful for . . .

OBJECTIVES Today my priority is . . .

TIME FOR MYSELF Today I want to . . .

HAPPINESS A beautiful thing that happened today was . . .

SUCCESS An obstacle I overcame today was . . .

MEMO TO SELF I would have improved my day if . . .

GRATITUDE Today I am grateful for . . .

OBJECTIVES Today my priority is . . .

TIME FOR MYSELF Today I want to . . .

HAPPINESS A beautiful thing that happened today was . . .

SUCCESS An obstacle I overcame today was . . .

MEMO TO SELF I would have improved my day if . . .

GRATITUDE Today I am grateful for . . .

OBJECTIVES Today my priority is . . .

TIME FOR MYSELF Today I want to . . .

HAPPINESS A beautiful thing that happened today was . . .

SUCCESS An obstacle I overcame today was . . .

MEMO TO SELF I would have improved my day if . . .

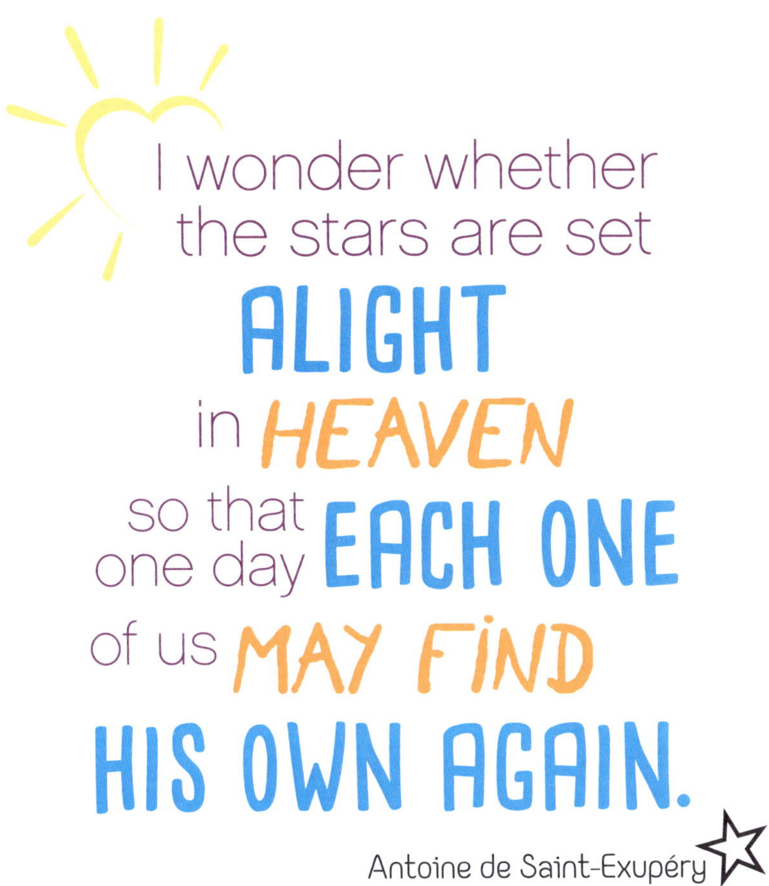

I wonder whether
the stars are set
ALIGHT
in HEAVEN
so that
one day EACH ONE
of us MAY FIND
HIS OWN AGAIN.
Antoine de Saint-Exupéry

GRATITUDE Today I am grateful for . . .

OBJECTIVES Today my priority is . . .

TIME FOR MYSELF Today I want to . . .

HAPPINESS A beautiful thing that happened today was . . .

SUCCESS An obstacle I overcame today was . . .

MEMO TO SELF I would have improved my day if . . .

GRATITUDE Today I am grateful for . . .

OBJECTIVES Today my priority is . . .

TIME FOR MYSELF Today I want to . . .

HAPPINESS A beautiful thing that happened today was . . .

SUCCESS An obstacle I overcame today was . . .

MEMO TO SELF I would have improved my day if . . .

GRATITUDE Today I am grateful for . . .

OBJECTIVES Today my priority is . . .

TIME FOR MYSELF Today I want to . . .

HAPPINESS A beautiful thing that happened today was . . .

SUCCESS An obstacle I overcame today was . . .

MEMO TO SELF I would have improved my day if . . .

SU MO TU WE TH FR SA

GRATITUDE Today I am grateful for . . .

OBJECTIVES Today my priority is . . .

TIME FOR MYSELF Today I want to . . .

HAPPINESS A beautiful thing that happened today was . . .

SUCCESS An obstacle I overcame today was . . .

MEMO TO SELF I would have improved my day if . . .

month day year

SU MO TU WE TH FR SA

GRATITUDE Today I am grateful for . . .

OBJECTIVES Today my priority is . . .

TIME FOR MYSELF Today I want to . . .

HAPPINESS A beautiful thing that happened today was . . .

SUCCESS An obstacle I overcame today was . . .

MEMO TO SELF I would have improved my day if . . .

GRATITUDE Today I am grateful for . . .

OBJECTIVES Today my priority is . . .

TIME FOR MYSELF Today I want to . . .

HAPPINESS A beautiful thing that happened today was . . .

SUCCESS An obstacle I overcame today was . . .

MEMO TO SELF I would have improved my day if . . .

SU MO TU WE TH FR SA

GRATITUDE Today I am grateful for . . .

OBJECTIVES Today my priority is . . .

TIME FOR MYSELF Today I want to . . .

HAPPINESS A beautiful thing that happened today was . . .

SUCCESS An obstacle I overcame today was . . .

MEMO TO SELF I would have improved my day if . . .

The foolish man
seeks happiness
in the DISTANCE,
the wise grows it
under his FEET.
James Oppenheim

GRATITUDE Today I am grateful for . . .

OBJECTIVES Today my priority is . . .

TIME FOR MYSELF Today I want to . . .

HAPPINESS A beautiful thing that happened today was . . .

SUCCESS An obstacle I overcame today was . . .

MEMO TO SELF I would have improved my day if . . .

GRATITUDE Today I am grateful for . . .

OBJECTIVES Today my priority is . . .

TIME FOR MYSELF Today I want to . . .

HAPPINESS A beautiful thing that happened today was . . .

SUCCESS An obstacle I overcame today was . . .

MEMO TO SELF I would have improved my day if . . .

SU MO TU WE TH FR SA

GRATITUDE Today I am grateful for . . .

OBJECTIVES Today my priority is . . .

TIME FOR MYSELF Today I want to . . .

HAPPINESS A beautiful thing that happened today was . . .

SUCCESS An obstacle I overcame today was . . .

MEMO TO SELF I would have improved my day if . . .

GRATITUDE Today I am grateful for . . .

OBJECTIVES Today my priority is . . .

TIME FOR MYSELF Today I want to . . .

HAPPINESS A beautiful thing that happened today was . . .

SUCCESS An obstacle I overcame today was . . .

MEMO TO SELF I would have improved my day if . . .

GRATITUDE Today I am grateful for . . .

OBJECTIVES Today my priority is . . .

TIME FOR MYSELF Today I want to . . .

HAPPINESS A beautiful thing that happened today was . . .

SUCCESS An obstacle I overcame today was . . .

MEMO TO SELF I would have improved my day if . . .

GRATITUDE Today I am grateful for . . .

OBJECTIVES Today my priority is . . .

TIME FOR MYSELF Today I want to . . .

HAPPINESS A beautiful thing that happened today was . . .

SUCCESS An obstacle I overcame today was . . .

MEMO TO SELF I would have improved my day if . . .

GRATITUDE Today I am grateful for . . .

OBJECTIVES Today my priority is . . .

TIME FOR MYSELF Today I want to . . .

HAPPINESS A beautiful thing that happened today was . . .

SUCCESS An obstacle I overcame today was . . .

MEMO TO SELF I would have improved my day if . . .

Our LIFE
is frittered away
by DETAIL.
Simplicity, simplicity,
SIMPLICITY!
Henry David Thoreau

GRATITUDE Today I am grateful for . . .

OBJECTIVES Today my priority is . . .

TIME FOR MYSELF Today I want to . . .

HAPPINESS A beautiful thing that happened today was . . .

SUCCESS An obstacle I overcame today was . . .

MEMO TO SELF I would have improved my day if . . .

SU MO TU WE TH FR SA

GRATITUDE Today I am grateful for . . .

OBJECTIVES Today my priority is . . .

TIME FOR MYSELF Today I want to . . .

HAPPINESS A beautiful thing that happened today was . . .

SUCCESS An obstacle I overcame today was . . .

MEMO TO SELF I would have improved my day if . . .

month

day

year

SU MO TU WE TH FR SA

GRATITUDE Today I am grateful for . . .

OBJECTIVES Today my priority is . . .

TIME FOR MYSELF Today I want to . . .

HAPPINESS A beautiful thing that happened today was . . .

SUCCESS An obstacle I overcame today was . . .

MEMO TO SELF I would have improved my day if . . .

GRATITUDE Today I am grateful for . . .

OBJECTIVES Today my priority is . . .

TIME FOR MYSELF Today I want to . . .

HAPPINESS A beautiful thing that happened today was . . .

SUCCESS An obstacle I overcame today was . . .

MEMO TO SELF I would have improved my day if . . .

SU MO TU WE TH FR SA

GRATITUDE Today I am grateful for . . .

OBJECTIVES Today my priority is . . .

TIME FOR MYSELF Today I want to . . .

HAPPINESS A beautiful thing that happened today was . . .

SUCCESS An obstacle I overcame today was . . .

MEMO TO SELF I would have improved my day if . . .

SU MO TU WE TH FR SA

GRATITUDE Today I am grateful for . . .

OBJECTIVES Today my priority is . . .

TIME FOR MYSELF Today I want to . . .

HAPPINESS A beautiful thing that happened today was . . .

SUCCESS An obstacle I overcame today was . . .

MEMO TO SELF I would have improved my day if . . .

GRATITUDE Today I am grateful for . . .

OBJECTIVES Today my priority is . . .

TIME FOR MYSELF Today I want to . . .

HAPPINESS A beautiful thing that happened today was . . .

SUCCESS An obstacle I overcame today was . . .

MEMO TO SELF I would have improved my day if . . .

Yesterday
I was CLEVER,
so I wanted to
change the world.
Today
I am WISE,
so I am changing
MYSELF.
Rumi

SU MO TU WE TH FR SA

GRATITUDE Today I am grateful for . . .

OBJECTIVES Today my priority is . . .

TIME FOR MYSELF Today I want to . . .

HAPPINESS A beautiful thing that happened today was . . .

SUCCESS An obstacle I overcame today was . . .

MEMO TO SELF I would have improved my day if . . .

SU MO TU WE TH FR SA

GRATITUDE Today I am grateful for . . .

OBJECTIVES Today my priority is . . .

TIME FOR MYSELF Today I want to . . .

HAPPINESS A beautiful thing that happened today was . . .

SUCCESS An obstacle I overcame today was . . .

MEMO TO SELF I would have improved my day if . . .

GRATITUDE Today I am grateful for . . .

OBJECTIVES Today my priority is . . .

TIME FOR MYSELF Today I want to . . .

HAPPINESS A beautiful thing that happened today was . . .

SUCCESS An obstacle I overcame today was . . .

MEMO TO SELF I would have improved my day if . . .

GRATITUDE Today I am grateful for . . .

OBJECTIVES Today my priority is . . .

TIME FOR MYSELF Today I want to . . .

HAPPINESS A beautiful thing that happened today was . . .

SUCCESS An obstacle I overcame today was . . .

MEMO TO SELF I would have improved my day if . . .

SU MO TU WE TH FR SA

GRATITUDE Today I am grateful for . . .

OBJECTIVES Today my priority is . . .

TIME FOR MYSELF Today I want to . . .

HAPPINESS A beautiful thing that happened today was . . .

SUCCESS An obstacle I overcame today was . . .

MEMO TO SELF I would have improved my day if . . .

247

GRATITUDE Today I am grateful for . . .

OBJECTIVES Today my priority is . . .

TIME FOR MYSELF Today I want to . . .

HAPPINESS A beautiful thing that happened today was . . .

SUCCESS An obstacle I overcame today was . . .

MEMO TO SELF I would have improved my day if . . .

GRATITUDE Today I am grateful for . . .

OBJECTIVES Today my priority is . . .

TIME FOR MYSELF Today I want to . . .

HAPPINESS A beautiful thing that happened today was . . .

SUCCESS An obstacle I overcame today was . . .

MEMO TO SELF I would have improved my day if . . .

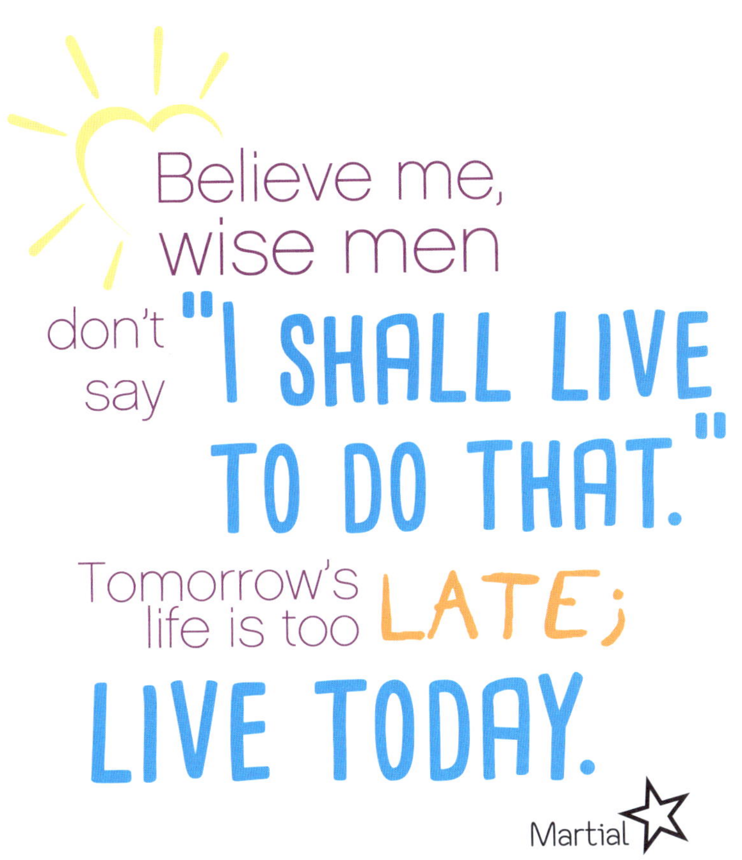

Believe me, wise men don't say "I SHALL LIVE TO DO THAT." Tomorrow's life is too LATE; LIVE TODAY.
Martial

CONGRATULATIONS!

You've completed six months of the Happiness Journal.

take a deep

BREATH
and
SMILE

HOW DID IT GO?

Take five minutes to reflect on how working on the journal changed you.

Were you able to write in the journal every day?

What benefits did you discover?

Did you learn something about yourself?
Did you find your own method to live each day in the best way possible?
How do you feel? Are you happier?

Twenty years from now
you won't be disappointed
by what you have done,
but by what you have not done.
So lift the anchor, leave the safe
harbor, take the wind in your sails.
Explore. Dream. Discover.

Mark Twain